FROM
CLOD BUSTER
TO CLOUD CHASER

FROM
CLOD BUSTER
TO CLOUD CHASER

BRIG. GEN. OSCAR A. HURT

TATE PUBLISHING
AND ENTERPRISES, LLC

Published by Tate Publishing & Enterprises, LLC
127 E. Trade Center Terrace | Mustang, Oklahoma 73064 USA
1.888.361.9473 | www.tatepublishing.com

Tate Publishing is committed to excellence in the publishing industry. The company reflects the philosophy established by the founders, based on Psalm 68:11,
"The Lord gave the word and great was the company of those who published it."

Book design copyright © 2014 by Tate Publishing, LLC. All rights reserved.
Cover design by Nikolai Purpura
Interior design by James Mensidor

Published in the United States of America

ISBN: 978-1-63122-824-7
1. Biography & Autobiography / Personal Memoirs
2. Biography & Autobiography / Military
14.06.20

Acknowledgment

Had it not been for the support and guidance so generously provided by Lt/Gen. Dan Druen, this book would never have been written. Dan's encouragement bolstered my desire to convey to readers, using the real events of my own life as an example, that dreams can indeed be made to come true.

I also want to thank my wife and our two sons whose continuing support and approval played an important part in buttressing my confidence.

I am deeply indebted to Janice Wheeler for graciously editing my text and critiquing the book's content. Also, thanks to Mick, Donna, Mary Ann, Susan, and my sister, Betty, whose appraisals of early drafts were a great help.

And to my grandson, Garek, I owe you one for taking time out of your busy schedule to design the splendid cover for this book.

CONTENTS

PROLOGUE

This book is written to support my firm belief that in this wonderful country of America, anyone can dream—and have reasonable hope that those dreams can be brought to fruition. My story is the cataloguing of events in the life of the son of a hired hand on a pig farm who became an air force officer and commercial pilot. It chronicles the experiences of a very bashful, unsophisticated kid who grew to be comfortable at Pentagon briefings and traveled to many of the major cities of the world. The story itself is not important unless the reader realizes that they, too, can live their dream. It isn't always easy. It requires decisiveness, courage, tenacity, self confidence, a bit of luck, a "leg up" once in a while, perhaps a bit of divine intervention, and frequently, some sacrifices.

As you read, you will note that there were many people in my life whose compassion, belief, support, and endorsement were crucial. I cannot possibly thank them enough (and, unfortunately, several of them are no longer with us).

My second objective in writing this book is to tell the story of a somewhat ragtag Air National Guard and Air Force Reserve system as it grew into a very solid partner of the active air force in building the finest fighting machine in the world.

I have written from memory, but the time frame is close, events are completely factual, and conversation quotes are reasonably accurate. I am fortunate to have served with so many wonderful people in the military. They came from broad economic, educational, and social backgrounds but they shared an unfettered love for their country and were willing to give their lives for that country.

THE FORMATIVE YEARS

Life for me began on a hot June day in 1923 on a pig farm in west central Iowa where my father was employed as a hired hand. I was born lucky. Mother and Dad were intelligent, industrious, and well disciplined. Both were excellent Icons.

Dad was born in the Ozarks and at the age of twenty began to dream of a different life. He did not own any form of transportation so he literally *walked* away from home in pursuit of that dream. He found employment as a salesman with the Barnum Book Company and quickly became one of the company's leading producers, earning enough money to attend medical school. However WWI and a hitch in the Navy put an end to both careers. After the war, Dad went back to his sales work, walking (he didn't own a car—not even a motorcycle) through northern Kansas and later, northern Iowa where he met my mother. They were soon married, and with but $5 to their name, they were happy to have a job—any job.

In 1927 my mother's father helped them find a small (120 acre) farm to rent in northwest Iowa and supplemented their meager savings with the funds necessary to start farming on their own. At the age of five, I started to school, walking the two miles each direction except during inclement weather when Dad or Mom would take me in our old open-curtain car.

Oscar, front row, 2nd from left Circa 1930

I also became responsible for helping feed the livestock and milk the cows. There were no children living near us, so I spent my spare time making crude models of cars and trucks out of scrap wood, and my sister and I would play with them in a shady spot in the yard. There was little or no money for toys, but this became a blessing in disguise because I developed skill in the use of wood and metal working tools along with the ability to entertain myself.

Hard work, frugality, and tenacity paid off; and in 1932, Dad was offered the rental of a somewhat run-down 360-acre farm with an excellent set of barns, sheds, and storage bins—ideal for expansion of farm activity to include feeding of livestock, pigs, and chickens. This move would involve tripling the need for machinery, help, and livestock. Again, funding of such an operation was a big problem. The owner of the 360-acre farm also owned the farm we were living on at the time and had the greatest respect and confidence in my parents' work ethic. He was also a banker in a nearby town and was willing to sponsor the new operation on a partnership basis. We moved to the new farm in the early winter of 1932. New machinery would cost more than my father could afford, so the winter was spent going to sales to find satisfactory used equipment. The big question was whether to select horse-drawn machinery or go for tractor power. He finally opted for a combination of the two.

In the early 1930s, a 360-acre farm entailed a lot of hired help. Planting, cultivation, harvesting, care of the horses, maintenance of the machinery, feeding of cattle and pigs for marketing, and milking of the cows (twice a day) made it essential that everyone pitch in to the best of their ability. As harvest approached in the summer of 1933, Dad was faced with the necessity to hire someone to drive the tractor to pull him as he operated a binder (used to cut and tie the oat stalks into bundles for drying and later separation of the grain from the stalk). Again, the need for austerity was factored into his decision to let me (now ten years old) drive the tractor. I was excited over the opportunity, but I was very small, and Mother was afraid I would fall off the tractor with the inevitable consequence. The binder was a large machine that would be trailing the tractor at a distance of about twenty feet. Mother was right—had I fallen off, there would have been no hope for me. However, Dad rigged a rope from the clutch pedal to his seat on the binder so that, if needed, he could stop the tractor. We got through the season without incident, and I had proven my ability to drive the tractor.

At the age of twelve, I was big enough to help in the fields on a full-time basis. This would save the cost of a hired hand during the cultivating season. The logical piece of equipment for me appeared to be a one-row cultivator pulled by two horses, but when I tried to operate it, we discovered that my legs were too short to reach the part of the equipment that guided the plows along the rows of corn. So it was back to the tractor where the plows were rigidly set, and you used tractor steering to control their path along the hills of corn. At the end of each trip through the field, I had to use a lever on each side of the tractor to lift the plows out of the ground for the turn. This was an approximate lift of fifty-five pounds, and over a period of time, I built some pretty good biceps.

I was also big enough to help in the shocking of the oats (placing the bundles in a small pile with the grain heads up to dry), and at fourteen, I was even big enough to handle a team of horses and a wagon to haul grain away from a threshing machine (used to separate the oat grain from the stalks) and unload the grain into a storage bin. I also took my turn in the house. Mother became pregnant with her third child and suffered with morning nausea, so I was diverted to the kitchen to prepare breakfast when Dad and our hired hand arose at 4:30 a.m. to milk the cows. I became rather proficient at making biscuits from scratch and frying eggs, bacon, sausage, and ham, and making gravy. In spite of all of this activity, there was time for scheduled high school sports, but neither the time nor transportation for the sandlot practice available to my peers in town. I was too small (four feet nine) to play basketball well, but my school had a small enrollment, so the coach did not have a large choice of players. In spite of that, there was some speculation that I would be nominated for outstanding guard in our senior year high school playoffs. It didn't happen. As for baseball, I don't think I ever got a hit in a baseball game; however, I had a very strong arm and a good fastball, so I served as pitcher once in a while, but lack of training limited my control and I was never a starting pitcher. The same strong arm served me well as an outfielder. Hits into center field were most often thrown to the second or third baseman or the shortstop for relay to the catcher to stop a runner trying to run home. However, I could throw a ball from center field and hit the catcher in the knees—much to the consternation of opposing team base runners that were playing against us for the first time.

In spite of my tender age while operating mechanized farm equipment, I had only one incident that could have been very serious. I was mowing the ditches around our farm one day with a tractor-mounted mower. This consisted of an eight-foot cutter bar that was mounted vey securely to the tractor draw bar (a heavy U-shaped piece of metal for hooking up to farm implements, i.e., plows, etc.). The cutter bar was approximately three-fourths of an inch thick, seven inches wide, and eight feet long and was made of high-quality steel. When not operating, the bar was stored in a vertical position on the right side of the drawbar and when in use would be lowered to the right to cut the grass. We had three tractors that the mower could be mounted on. Two of them were equipped with a six-foot wheel and tire and one of them with a five-foot wheel and tire (this information is critical to my story). On this particular day, the mower was mounted on the tractor with the taller wheel and tire. As I got to a portion of the ditch that had steep sides and a narrow valley between, I noted that the tractor was a bit light on the uphill side, but not to worry, I had mowed the same ditch about a month earlier. Unfortunately, I did not remember that on the previous occasion, we had used the tractor with the shorter wheel and tire, which provided a lower center of gravity and a more stable platform. Sure enough, moments later, the tractor rolled in the direction of the cutter bar. I made an attempt to jump in the direction of the roll, hoping to clear the machine. I hit the bank on the other side of the narrow ditch, and before I could scramble out of the way, the left wheel hit me in the back, knocking me to the ground. But this was my lucky day because the cutter bar hit its vertical stop and acted as a spring to stop and reverse the tractor's roll. In the second or two before the dead weight of the tractor could overpower the cutter bar, I had scrambled to safety. I speak of luck but have no doubt that it can be spelled "divine intervention."

I graduated from high school at age sixteen, and in August 1941, I left home to study aeronautical engineering at Parks Air College in East St. Louis, Illinois. It was a real challenge as I was dealing with a completely foreign vocabulary (vertical stabilizer, rudder, flaps, elevators, power curve, lift, drag, induced drag, parasite drag, ailerons). None of these words related in any way to "tractor, combine, cultivate" (common farm vernacular) but they began to be a part of my daily routine. Add to that the fact that I had never been away from home before for any appreciable period of time and I began to view my corner of the world differently. Needless to say the sights, sounds, and activity in St. Louis, Missouri, were an education in themselves for an eighteen year old farm boy.

WWII broke out in December, and I went home for the holidays intending to enlist in the army as a pilot. Dad was agreeable, but he had purchased another farm and asked if I would consider staying home for one summer to help get his enlarged farming operation under way. I agreed, and we farmed 560 acres with the help of one hired hand. This was a rather large operation for that time, especially in view of the fact that we used some of our machinery to take on work for our neighbors. In the late fall of 1942, I suffered a severe ear infection and ultimately underwent mastoid surgery. It disqualified me for service as an army pilot. I accepted an agricultural deferment and subsequent deferment renewals from military service until the late summer of 1945. At that time, I was selected for the draft. I requested and was granted a ninety-day deferment to finish the harvest; however, Japan surrendered in September of 1945, and the draft was terminated.

We sold our farming operation in 1946 and opened an Oldsmobile franchise in Spencer, Iowa. New cars were scarce, and the manufacturers favored the existing dealers whose service departments had supported them during the war even though there were no cars to sell. Used cars were pretty well worn out, and about the only customers and mechanics available were those who were dissatisfied with their current relationships. It made for a very frustrating operation, and as a consequence, we sold the business and began to manufacture a luggage trailer we had designed. Unfortunately, it had a fatal engineering design flaw, which we were unable to correct, and the business went into bankruptcy in late 1947.

Dad then opened a feed, seed, and fertilizer business, but start-up income was minimal. I decided to try my hand at sales and went to work for The Vita Craft Company in cookware sales. Very quickly, I found that I didn't really like selling. Living in a hotel and eating all my meals at restaurants was a totally foreign and rather lonely life. It soon became apparent to me that I needed to look elsewhere for a career. My only real success had been in farming, but I didn't want to go back to that. The dilemma was that I didn't have the funds to strike out on my own, and I couldn't see myself working for someone else. I was twenty-four years old, and it was obvious there were too many loose ends in my life.

THE BEGINNING OF A NEW CAREER

As 1948 began to play out, I found myself taking stock of my life. The Korean situation was heating up and might very well result in another major conflict. I knew that if the United States became involved in a war with Korea, I would be a prime candidate for induction into one of the services. I was the right age, I was single, and my health was excellent. Surgery had corrected my ear problem, and the infections were gone. In July of 1948, the air force announced that they were accepting applications for pilot training. I decided to give it a try. I passed the initial screening and was told to report to Denver, Colorado, for cadet classification testing. I soon learned that this series of tests were known as a *Stanine Profile* and consisted of a written comprehension test, map reading, and a series of psychomotor evaluations to determine physical coordination and performance under stress. There would also be an interview with a psychiatrist. Wow! What was a country boy to do? It was overwhelming. However, nothing ventured, nothing gained, so I plunged into the program and gave it my best.

I had learned that whenever you take an exam, it is usually best to first answer all the questions that are relatively easy and then go back to the hard ones. This was a big help on one of the tests, which was clearly designed with the expectation that no one could answer all questions in the time allocated, and scoring would be based on the percentage of correct answers you completed. The two days were a blur, and when the testing was complete, I was advised to go home and await the results. If I passed the Stanine Profile, I would be notified, and reporting instructions would follow.

I was accepted. However, the application process, security clearance, physical and mental testing, notification, and travel had consumed so much time that I would not be able to make my class reporting date, and this would be my only shot because my age (now twenty-five) would disqualify me for any subsequent class. Fortunately, I was given a two-week late-arrival waiver.

My basic flight training was to be at Randolph Field in San Antonio, Texas. The twenty-four-hour bus ride from northwest Iowa allowed more than enough time to ponder the life I was leaving and contemplate what my new life was going to be like. I had thoroughly enjoyed the days on the farm. It had been a disciplined life in that work in the fields, care of the livestock, and maintenance and improvement of the farmstead had all been part of the big picture, but each obligation demanded priority. Recreational activities became a possibility only when everything else had been done. In many ways, life was simple—you did what needed to be done when the need arose. My new life was going to be much more rigidly structured. There would be rigid schedules and timetables over which I would have no control or option. However, the opportunity to fly those wonderful machines far outweighed any inconvenience I could visualize.

I had been fairly adept at handling mechanized equipment, cars, tractors, and trucks; and I believed that those skills would carry over into pilot training. In any event, I was now on my way to being an air force pilot, and that vision had been with me from the time I was five years old.

I had previously accumulated about 175 hours of flying at a local airport, and all of those flights had gone well. Still, this was in no way a precursor to the rigid training required of an air force pilot. My high school academic scores had been fairly good, and math was one of my better subjects. However, a small-town high school graduate (fifty-two total students) going up against college grad classmates certainly would not be a shoo-in. (I would soon learn that one of my classmates was a Harvard graduate). In any event I was committed so it was time to "get on with it." It had been a long day, and we were well into the night when a fitful sleep finally shut down my wandering mind and allowed me to get some rest.

The bus rolled into the San Antonio Greyhound station promptly at the scheduled 7:00 a.m. hour (I had met my first air force schedule). Would the promised transportation be there? Sure enough, as I stepped off the bus and into the terminal, I spotted two men in military uniform. I approached them, gave them my name, and asked if they were there to pick me up. Their reply was "Yes sir, Mr. Hurt. Grab your bag, and we'll take you to the base for processing" amazed me because it was the first time anyone had ever called me mister. "Mr. Hurt" was surely my dad! But "Mister," it turns out, is also the military address for an aviation cadet. I did not realize it at the moment but it was more than that, it was a subtle introduction to military formality and courtesy which would dominate the rest of my life. We immediately embarked on the fifteen-mile drive to Randolph Field, and as we entered the base, I was impressed with the immaculately trimmed drive and the majestic Taj Mahal lookalike building (base headquarters) sitting at the end of the drive.

Randolph AFB Taj Mahal

I would soon be advised by upperclassmen that the Taj Mahal held ten thousand gallons of tutti-frutti ice cream for the upperclassmen. As ridiculous as this was,

I quickly recognized it as a "foot stomper" and made a mental note never to forget it.

Processing took the better part of the next four hours. One of the things I learned was that aviation cadets *could not be married*. What a quandary! I had been single when I submitted my application for training, so I had not falsified any records. I had been dating VI, and unaware of the marriage restriction, we decided to get married while waiting for the air force's decision. We were married in Santa Monica, California, in a quiet ceremony with only our parents and my sister aware of the event. Immediately after the ceremony, I had to return to Spencer, Iowa, because my bus ticket to San Antonio had been issued from that city. Should I tell the air force that I had not known of the regulation and hope for some form of exception, or should we just keep it quiet? Finally, I remembered that someone once told me that if you have dug a hole for yourself and want to crawl out of it, you have to stop digging. So I decided to keep my lip buttoned and "go for it." When the processing was completed, I was taken to my barracks and carefully briefed on the proper way to display clothing (shirts left shoulder out, two fingers between hangers, etc., and something about white glove inspections). Our rooms were approximately twenty feet square with a double-deck bunk bed, very austere, with a sink in the room; lavatory and showers were down the hall. I was given the two or three remaining hours of the day to relax and told to meet the morning formation at 6:00 a.m. However, there was a bit of a glitch: my uniforms were not available, so I would have to wear my civilian clothing. I did not realize it at the time, but this "small" problem was going to create a lot of discomfort the next day. I went to bed early and again slept rather fitfully.

I was awakened the next morning by the blaring sound of a horn (call that a bugle, mister, and it is blowing "Reveille" [military morning bugle "wake-up" call]) and a mad rush of classmates into their uniforms. I quickly dressed in my civvies (dark blue pinstripe suit, white shirt, and flaming red tie) and fell out for the morning formation. Wow! I stood out like a turkey in a flock of chickens. I may not be the proverbial "sharpest knife in the drawer," but it took less than a nanosecond for me to realize that the reporting waiver, which allowed me to join my class two weeks late, had suddenly become a huge albatross around my neck. My classmates had already been on board for two weeks. Their initial indoctrination was over, and they had fallen out for the first time in uniform.

My indoctrination was just beginning. I've never seen so many upperclassmen swarm like a hive of bees to get at the "new guy." They were all intent on ensuring that I knew how to say "yes, sir," "no, sir," and "no excuse, sir." They were also determined that I knew how to stand, where to look, *and* the number of gallons of ice cream that were in the Taj Mahal and who it belonged to. (What a bunch of baloney. I was twenty-five, had enjoyed some success in business and had lived through failure. Most of these "kids" were in their early twenties, and apparently none had ever learned that if you get that close and that loud in another man's face, someone is going to come away with a bloody nose.) Fortunately, reason quickly caught up with me, and while I didn't understand the need for these "games," I accepted that they were part of the training. I had already lived through much worse, and I was determined that no one was going to do me in. This decision was fortified a couple of weeks later when I saw a cadet who had been a staff sergeant in the army actually break down under the pressure. My heart bled for the poor guy because it was the end of an aviation career for him.

FLIGHT TRAINING

The academic part of flight training at Randolph field was not as difficult as I thought it would be. I rather enjoyed the math and some of the military subjects. A month after starting academics came the *big day*—we were headed for the flight line and flight instructor assignment. We were going to be flying the AT-6.

The "T-6" had been an advanced trainer at the end of WWII, but after the war, the air force decided to make it a basic trainer. Advanced trainers would be the B-25 (for multi-engine) or F-51 for single-engine.

The T-6 was a great single-engine basic trainer—600 HP, low wing, tail dragger (airplanes with a wheel at the rear of the airplane rather than the front are often called tail draggers), fully aerobatic, and cruised about 155 mph. Each instructor was assigned two students. My instructor was a Lt. S. He was low-key, quiet, and very pleasant, so I was pleased with the assignment.

Standard procedure was for the four-hour training period to be broken up into two two-hour periods. The first student would start the aircraft, complete his training period, taxi into the parking area, and disembark from the airplane while the engine was running. The second student would slip into the cockpit, taxi out, complete his training for the day, taxi in, and shut down. This procedure rarely varied except when students were scheduled for progress checks (somewhat of a misnomer because a progress check was a specially scheduled ride with one of the line supervisors, and frequently it was the precursor to elimination). I felt fairly comfortable with my flight performance, so I was not apprehensive one day when Lt. S called over the interphone as we taxied in from the first period and said, "Go ahead and shut it down, I feel like a Coke, and I'll buy you one." That was fine with me—Coca-Cola was not my favorite drink, but he was buying. We sat on the curb at the flight line for a bit making small talk when he turned to me and said, "Hurt, do you really want to fly?" I was dumfounded but quickly responded with the absolute truth: "I've never wanted anything more in my life." His next words were "Well, you seem to have a bit of an attitude." I had no idea what he was referring to, but I responded almost reflexively, "I love to fly, but this class system hazing is a problem for me. I've got kids spewing saliva in my face, and they aren't even dry behind the ears. I've been in and out of business, and this isn't a game for me." His response to my sudden outburst was, "Yeah, I can understand how you feel," and shortly thereafter, "Well, I better get back to work." I didn't fully realize it at the time, but there, in approximately two minutes, my whole career in the air force had dangled by a thread, and *but for the grace of a very compassionate man, my life would have ended up as something totally different.* To this day, tears come to my eyes when I think of that moment.

Flight training seemed to go well, academics were doable, and the day-to-day routine was fairly comfortable. There had been one brush with the demerit system (demerits were a negative report for infractions of cadet rules). After our indoctrination, we were given "open post" (freedom to go into town) during certain hours on the weekend. One critical rule was that we had to be back in quarters by 2000 hours on Sunday night. No problem. The Gunter hotel in downtown San Antonio provided a special watering hole for the aviation cadets, and I would put in an appearance before going on to spend time with my wife who had joined me in San Antonio, found a job, and shared a nice efficiency apartment with a mother and daughter on the edge of town. On my first visit, I returned to quarters almost one half hour early (or so I thought). I was actually late because of my lack of experience with the twenty-four-hour clock. I misconstrued 2000 hours as 10:00 p.m.; of course it would be 8:00 p.m., so I was an hour and a half late. Woe is me—this infraction cost me four hours on the ramp (the cement area in front of one of the hangers), walking off the penalty (pacing back and forth in a military manner). Not really a lot of fun, but it was going to be worse than I expected. The designated military uniform for walking demerits was class A. Somehow I missed that salient point (after all, this was my first offense), and I reported wearing the "uniform of the day." Fortunately, it was misting, so we reported wearing raincoats fully buttoned to the throat. Shortly after reporting, I realized I was *out of uniform* (nobody else knew because of the buttoned raincoat). It was probably the first time in my life that I literally implored the good Lord to keep that mist coming. If it stopped, raincoats would come off, and I could only imagine what the penalty would be. More than that, the cadet program had little tolerance for goof-ups, and identification with that kind of group was a major liability at best.

Two months after starting flight training, we reached the aerobatic stage. Every red-blooded pilot wannabe approached this phase with great anticipation and expectation. I was no exception, but I was also somewhat worried. I had experienced one incident of airsickness during my private civilian lessons; would this be a problem again? (It turned out that it was, in spades.) Inability to overcome air-sickness was a one-way ticket back to civilian life. It would be quick and brutally final. On my first aerobatic flight, I quickly became ill, but I held on, and we got through some maneuvers. I could handle the coordinated maneuvers (loops, chandelles, Cuban eights), but slow rolls in the T-6 filled the cockpit with fuel fumes and made me very nauseous. I finally realized my breakfast was about to return and reached for the microphone on the cockpit sidewall. I just couldn't do any more. Before I could squeeze the transmit button, it clicked, and there was the voice of Lt. S, saying, "Boy, I was at a big party last night, and I've had enough. Open your canopy so I can get some air back here and take me home." (It is significant to note that the T-6 had two cockpits in tandem, and the flight instructor occupied the rear cockpit. Since each cockpit had a canopy of its own, if he really needed air, he could have opened his own canopy.) There were three or four more flights wherein he complained about his "big party" but perseverance prevailed and we finally got him through *my aerobatics*. Again, *I know that I owe my entire military career to this magnanimous officer.*

In February of 1949, air force regulations were amended to allow aviation cadets to be married. My wife and I went to a local judge and performed our vows again. Since married cadets were given an additional spousal pay allowance, we submitted the necessary paperwork to augment our income.

Basic training at Randolph Field finally came to an end, and school selection for advanced training began. I would have given a critical part of my anatomy to fly the F-51, but better judgment prevailed. In addition to the air-sickness problem, the fighter program was, in my opinion, more suitable for younger, unmarried pilots. After all, I was the old man of the group (I would graduate one month before the age limit would have disqualified my application). Also, I was ready to raise a family, and in 1949, bombardment and airlift experience seemed to predominate in the major command headquarters. I had known some pilot trainees who were unceremoniously dumped into civilian life at the end of WWII, and it occurred to me that a multi-engine background might be more beneficial if I were to find myself in similar circumstances and looking to the airlines for employment. This proved to be, at least partially, an error in judgment as fighter operations thereafter began to predominate, and I believe that most of today's senior commanders have combat fighter experience in their background. However, the civilian airline employment part of it did work for me—but more about that later.

I went on to advanced training at Barksdale AFB in Bossier City, Louisiana (and those annoying upperclassmen were gone!). The B-25 (a light twin-engine bomber) had served in both the Pacific and Europe. It had great single-engine performance, and I thoroughly enjoyed my "stick time." (Flight time, where the pilot is hand flying the aircraft versus use of the auto pilot or performing co-pilot duties.) My wife had followed me to this assignment, found a great apartment with a delightful local family, and was also hired by the Base Exchange (very much like a civilian general store) at Barksdale AFB. Not only could I stop in for a visit at the BX, but she was known and very well liked by my compatriots. We had much more time to share, and for the first time in months, the ever-present pressure and necessity for secrecy was gone.

Meanwhile a small problem was developing on the flight line. My flight instructor could reasonably be described as the south end of a north-bound horse. Fortunately, I was able to put those feelings aside for the sake of my career, and my advanced flight training progress went well. I did not have to experience the displeasure of a microphone rap across the knuckles, as my unfortunate teammate often did. In spite of it all, both he and I graduated in September of 1949 as members of Class 49C. I have no substantiation but have been told that there were approximately 2,200 applicants for the class, approximately 1,200 were selected for training, and approximately 600 of us graduated from various advanced training centers in the United States. Somewhere in my records is the statement that I graduated, thirty-third out of a group of 101 in our advanced multi-engine class at Barksdale. I was satisfied but never forgot for a minute that it all came about through the grace of that very compassionate basic flight training instructor at Randolph Field.

Training was over. I was now officially one of the world's finest—a pilot in the United States Air Force. My graduation and the pinning of those wings and second lieutenant bars was a great occasion. Both my parents and my wife's drove the nine-hundred-plus miles to share the occasion. My wife and I would have two weeks to go wherever and do whatever we wanted. We chose to return to our hometown, kick back, and enjoy some barbecue before I reported for my first active duty assignment.

ACTIVE DUTY

Active duty assignments seemed unpredictable at best. I had applied for assignment to the Military Airlift Command (the Air Forces' transportation service) but instead wound up assigned to one of our basic pilot training bases (James Connally AFB in Waco, Texas) as a basic flight instructor. This was a disappointment, but in retrospect, it may have been a blessing. Several graduates of class 49C lost their lives in crashes around the United States and Europe. The number of accidents was of such magnitude that we became known as "49-crash," and it seemed clear that our instrument training (controlling the aircraft using instruments in the cockpit as reference rather than using visual cues outside the cockpit) had been deficient.

Flight instruction could be rewarding, but it could also be rather dull and routine. Even so, as an instructor, you could not avoid learning something new as you taught primary flight principles over and over again. Occasionally, you learned a strategic lesson out of sheer necessity. Such was the case one day in May 1950, when the training squadron decided to put together a massive forty-eight-ship (T-6) formation and flyby for the city of Waco. Our intrepid operations commander (Major K) was to be the lead. All went well until our leader found a solid overcast had formed over our landing area. At the same time, he needed to return to base because the flyby was complete, and the weather forecast was calling for continued deteriorating conditions. Major K finally spotted a hole in the overcast; it was small and the cloud layer was fairly thick. No problem. He decided to suddenly reduce his power and dive through the hole without alerting the formation of the abrupt power change and expected the forty-seven wingmen to follow. From my position near the rear right side of the formation, it suddenly resembled a flock of ducks falling out of the sky as trailing aircraft began to overrun the lead. I had not been trained for this, but it was obvious that I needed to cut my power and throw out the landing gear and flaps—anything to slow airspeed and avoid overrunning the aircraft ahead of me. If that wasn't enough, I could slide out to the right. Fortunately I was able to hold a "loose" position, and we all made it through the hole without incident. The mission debriefing was one of the most vigorous and thorough I would experience throughout my entire career.

I quickly found that basic flight instruction involved a lot more than just showing a trainee how to do a maneuver, critiquing his work and repeating the procedure until he got it right. My first student, Mr. G, was an intelligent, modest, sincere young man with an intense desire to learn to fly. However, it soon became apparent that he lacked confidence in himself and was hesitant to make changes in control movements and power settings essential to a specific maneuver. I began to encourage him to overshoot and exaggerate his corrections in an effort to bracket proper settings or control movements. This was contrary to my usual instruction that called for smooth, gentle adjustments, but it began to show results. As he gained confidence, his proficiency rapidly improved, and he completed basic training satisfactorily.

Mr. W was completely the reverse. He was a strong student, handled the aircraft well, and knew when his performance had been particularly good. (I could always tell because he would turn his head and give me a big grin.) On one occasion, when we were departing for a supervised cross-country flight, he made a sharp turn out of traffic. One characteristic of the T-6 trainer was that a sharp rolling and climbing turn could tumble the heading gyro (which gave us information as to our direction of travel). I suspected that it might have happened in his turn, so I peeked over his shoulder; sure enough, the gyro had tumbled and was about twenty degrees off from what his actual heading should have read. This was an opportunity to trim his sails a bit. As our flight progressed, I occasionally queried him with questions designed to confuse him as to his location. After about fifteen minutes, I asked him to tell me exactly where we were. He could not do so. There were several procedures he could use to relocate his position, but none of those worked. As a last resort, he made the choice to fly over a town, look for a railroad station, and fly low enough to identify the town by reading the name off the station facility. When he completed his flyby, I asked him what the name said, and his reply was "freight house." I scornfully suggested that he find the town of *Freight House* on his map and then head for home. It had been a tough day for him, and when we landed, I discreetly leaked news of his search for Freight House, Texas. This cooled Mr. W down for a while, but he persevered and graduated with well above the average skills of his classmates.

My last student was Mr. G, a black cadet who was obviously under tremendous pressure to be successful. He was tense, made quick, erratic, uncoordinated movements, and frequently reacted too swiftly to properly assess the best course of action for a specific situation. I sat and talked with him several times, trying to assure him that he was going to be all right and explaining that he needed to slow down a bit. I also tried to find ways to praise or compliment him. I left before his training was complete and with considerable misgivings as to his future. Unfortunately, I learned a few weeks later that he had washed out of the program.

In early 1951, I noted that the Air Force Pilot Instructor School (known as PIS) had relocated its headquarters to Craig AFB at Selma, Alabama. The expansion created new openings for instructor personnel, and although I realized that I was "a new kid on the block," the possibility of a prestigious new assignment was appealing. Basic training was a bit boring, and nothing ventured would mean nothing gained. That old saying paid off because my application was approved, and my wife and I headed for the Deep South. It was there that I met some of the finest instructors, both flight and academic, that I have ever worked with. While I much preferred my flight duties, the academics forced me to delve much more deeply into the technical aspects of flying and also taught me to speak before a group, something that had been completely foreign and rather awkward for "an old farm boy." Because of the localized nature of our flying, cross-country navigation proficiency was prone to suffer. To compensate for this, we were encouraged to check out one of the base aircraft (C-47, a twin-engine transport, and B-25, a twin-engine bomber) for cross-country navigational training. I was " instructor pilot" qualified in the B-25, so, one weekend, I decided to take a training flight up into the Midwest. My crew was another PIS instructor and two of the school's students. None of them were qualified in the B-25, so there would be a lot of training accomplished during the weekend. I put the PIS instructor in the seat first because he was working on being checked out in the aircraft and also wanted to be dropped in Terre Haute, Indiana. No problem, as night navigation and a night landing at a strange field would then be accomplished. We dropped the PIS instructor off, completing the first leg, and departed for our RON (remain over night) base. The flight was long, and I knew the students were anxious for stick time, so about forty minutes into the flight, I decided to relinquish my seat to one of them. During the seat change, the student stumbled in the dark and grabbed a handle on the overhead to keep from falling. That "handle" was the overhead escape hatch release—which promptly served its purpose and released the escape hatch. The noise and rush of air toward the lowered pressure outside the aircraft created more confusion as we hastily completed the seat change. I had no more than gotten my feet firmly on the fuselage floor than I realized that some sort of white material was billowing and moving toward the open hatch. Suddenly, sheer terror engulfed me as I realized my parachute had somehow been released, and it was about to get taught in the slipstream. Had that happened, it would have yanked me through the (twenty-four-inch by thirty-inch) hatch opening and would, no doubt, have broken every bone in my body. It would also have left two souls on board at night in a B-25, an aircraft in which they had absolutely no experience. There is no doubt that I hold the speed record for getting out of a backpack parachute. Fortunately, I was able to gather the parachute material and keep it from exiting the airplane. Once again, it seemed to me that the good Lord had been at my elbow and must have something in mind for me. I had also learned to never, ever, *under any circumstances*, allow an airplane to be at the mercy of an inexperienced pilot.

One of the major functions at Craig AFB was the training of civilian pilots hired by the Air Force to instruct at the civilian contract schools which were opening to help train the large numbers of pilots required by the Air Force in the fifties. I was somewhat surprised one day to find a friend from my hometown on the roster of a new class. I knew that the friend had been in cadet training in WWII but had been one of those released when the war ended. I did not know how much training he had gotten before release so I asked his instructor to keep me posted as to his progress. Soon after the class started flying the instructor approached me, advising that my friend was having difficulty with landings and he was going to have to schedule him for a progress check. This was bad news because instructors did not schedule the progress check until they were of the opinion the student could not complete training successfully.

I was deeply concerned but there wasn't much I could do. His instructor was well qualified so that was not the problem. It was time for a major decision. I knew a second discharge from the Air Force was going to be almost catastrophic for my friend because of other events taking place in his life. I decided to see if I could check out one of our trainers for a navigation training trip. If approved, it was my plan to take my friend to an airport about 150 miles from our base and give him some very concentrated landing practice. My request was approved for the coming weekend. I had coordinated the plan with the instructor and he had agreed to hold off on the progress check until he had a chance to evaluate our success/failure on the following Monday.

The flight went well. I got my navigation training and we accomplished almost three hours of concentrated landing practice. I was fairly comfortable with our progress and we returned to our home base. Fortunately, the instructor was also satisfied and my friend went on to complete flight training and spent several years as a civilian Air Force flight instructor at a base in Texas.

I was very pleased to have been able to pass on the "leg up" that my basic flight instructor had so generously given me. There had been no sacrifice or violation of air force standards, regulations, or safety. My friend had been given a chance and he was able to capitalize on it. We were successful because we didn't accept what appeared to be inevitable.

North American B-25

TROOP CARRIER/ COMBAT CARGO

I was enjoying my work as a pilot instructor at Craig AFB, and it was definitely a great learning opportunity for me. Still, the Korean War was going on, and I wanted some of the action. I also knew that if I was going to be a career officer, I needed some combat experience in my personnel file. So I began checking the personnel releases for openings in the Korean theater. Finally, one did appear. The air force was looking for someone to fill an assignment as a twin-engine pilot in FEAF (Far East Air Force). I believed this would be B-26 light bombardment in Korea, so I submitted my application, and it was subsequently approved.

Very soon, I was on my way to Korea. Processing outbound at San Francisco was smooth and efficient. Medical and personnel records were brought up to date, and we were loaded on a MATS (Military Air Transport Service) airplane for the long haul across the Pacific to Tokyo, where we would again be processed—this time into the Far East Command jurisdiction. I soon learned that the air force flew more than one type of twin-engine airplane in the Korean theater. One of them was the C-46 (a fairly large and, I thought, ungainly twin-engine transport) and THAT was to be my assignment. I had already learned that life didn't always flow smoothly, so one needs to "suck it up and get on with it."

File:C-46 Commando.jpg
From Wikipedia, the free encyclopedia

Curtiss C-46 (Cmmando)

The airplane had served magnificently hauling cargo over the "Hump" during WWI, so I reasoned that it must have some redeeming features. And it did. I ultimately accumulated approximately 1,200 hours in the aircraft as pilot, instructor pilot, and squadron check pilot, and I learned to respect the Wright R-2600 power plant, one of the best reciprocating engines I ever advanced a throttle on. Pilot, Twenty-Fifth Troop

Carrier Squadron, was my assignment at Brady AFB in southern Japan. At that time in the air force, the large, four-engine MATS airplanes were used to move cargo and troops from the United States to Japan; the troop carriers (smaller twin-engine transports) would pick up the cargo/crews at Tokyo and move these to the smaller Korean bases and airstrips. Brady AFB had an old airstrip that was "paved" with PSP (pierced steel planking—heavy metal pieces that could be interlocked to form a firm landing area quickly). Our runway was on a small strip of land bordered by water on both ends of the runway. The runway length was considered minimal for a C-46 under normal dry conditions. PSP was notorious in that, any time it rained it could accurately be described as slippery as a sheet of ice. The prevailing approach was over a short sea wall, and during the next year, the squadron would lose three aircraft—one on the approach end with a sheered gear and two standing on their noses on the roll-out end of the runway.

The squadron was responsible for delivery of "combat cargo" (no combat that I could see, but a lot of cargo) up and down the chain of Japanese Islands and throughout all of the Korean bases south of the thirty-eighth parallel (the division between North and South Korea). It was also responsible for flare drops north of the thirty-eighth, hospital evacuation, deceased removal, and courier runs (much like a scheduled airline operation) in Korea and also in Japan. My PIS background soon caught up with me, and I was designated the group training officer. Much of my time was spent teaching the technical side of instrument flying, squadron flight checks and yeoman instructor work. When time permitted, I also took my turn on the Korean courier run.

Korea, Courier Route

One of the courier flights left Brady at 7:00 p.m. crossed the Tsushima Straights (the water area between

Japan and South Korea) and stopped at Pusan (at the southeast corner of South Korea) to offload mail, cargo, and passengers. The next stop was Seoul where fuel would be loaded for the return to Japan by way of Anyang (at the northeast corner of South Korea) and Pohang (on the east coast, about one-half of the way down the peninsula). The forty-minute leg from Seoul to Anyang was about forty miles south of the thirty-eighth parallel. While it was fascinating to observe the constant spectacular fireworks from the mortar and artillery shelling, it was also pretty disconcerting to sit there, safe and warm in the airplane, knowing each burst of light could herald the death of some young man and pain for a loving family and friends.

On one of my first flights, I was crewed with another squadron newcomer to make a run across the Tsushima Straits up to Seoul, Korea, and return down the west coast of Korea and back to Japan. Initially, all went well. We reached Seoul, offloaded our cargo, filed clearance papers, and departed southbound for our first checkpoint on the final leg of the journey. Upon reaching it, I leaned across to my copilot (Lt. B) and asked what our new heading was. His reply was *samo-samo* (continue on our current heading). This was a bit unusual; checkpoints usually involved minor heading changes at least. However Lt. B's very positive response negated any doubts that I had, and we proceeded on the *samo-samo* heading. This was a thirty-minute leg. After about fifteen minutes, our navigation radios were unreliable at best. This was not particularly disturbing because the old C-46 "coffee grinder" navigation receiver reception was not that good if you were beyond shouting distance from the transmitter. Another fifteen minutes passed, and we should have arrived at our next checkpoint. We still had no navigation reception. More disconcerting was our inability to raise anyone on our communication radios. It was long past time to recheck our charts, especially that last checkpoint. Once we did check, our error was quickly apparent. We should have made a twenty-degree heading correction, and failing to do so, we were now well out over the Yellow Sea, west of Korea. Since radar coverage was not available in that area, we were pretty much on our own to solve the problem and find our way home. A further study of our charts showed that we needed to make a major left turn, with the expectation that we would eventually pick up radio reception to confirm our estimated position. But…was it possible that we had flown so far off course that we were outside the South Korean coastal defense system? If so, would we be seen as an invading enemy aircraft? Luckily, we did have one major asset at our disposal. The air force had an excellent fleet of F-94s on defensive alert in Japan. They could be airborne within two or three minutes, and their onboard radar could spot an aircraft miles away. What should we do? Seeking their help would be embarrassing to say the least. However, the obvious quickly became apparent; dumping a C-46 in the waters off the west cost of Japan would be considerably more embarrassing. I swallowed my pride, made the call, and we continued on our heading. About ten minutes later, I was startled to see a blaze of light pull up under my left wing slightly beyond the propeller arc, just as a friendly voice came over the headset assuring me all was well. A minor heading correction, and fifty minutes of time should put us right over the center of "Brady Air Patch." Our friend stayed with us for about five minutes, and then, after receiving our assurance that we could now handle things, he peeled off to the left and pulled "up, up, and away." What a beautiful sight.

On another evening, I departed southern Japan for the Korean bases. Even though there was a weather front approaching Korea, my first stop was routine—as was the briefing, planning, and departure on the next leg for K-9 (Seoul, Korea). About twenty minutes into the flight, I received a call from operations advising that all of Korea had gone below landing minimums. The only available alternate was Tokyo, and it was expected to "tank" before I could get there. There was one other small problem: I didn't have enough fuel to make Tokyo anyway. The only feasible plan was to continue to Seoul and hope that their ground-controlled approach (GCA) system and I could get the airplane to a landing position on the runway. (GCA is a radar facility that can direct an airplane, both as to azimuth and elevation, on a final approach to an airport.) In any event, landing was going to be tough because the ceiling and visibility at K-9 was presently listed as zero/zero (cloud or fog condition is lying on the runway—no clearance between the ground and base of the cloud). Once again, extraordinary good luck prevailed, and as I was passing over a base approximately fifteen minutes south of Seoul, it suddenly reported a ceiling (cloud base) of eight hundred feet and visibility of four miles. We immediately diverted and landed without incident.

I mentioned that the C-46 had a pair of excellent power plants. Some of the aircraft also had a set of very bad propellers—bad, because they had the rare potential for going to full flat pitch. This is a condition in which the propeller does not bite into the slipstream and propel the aircraft forward. Instead, the propeller rotates at high speed, becoming a virtual flat wall of resistance to air passage around the engine and wing and creating a drag on the airplane that renders flight control (of even an empty airplane) impossible. Instant and precise corrective action is imperative, and even then, it is not always successful. On one occasion, the North Koreans were badly overrunning a Republic of South Korea contingent, and casualties were severe. I was assigned to air evacuation duty. The situation was so severe that we would taxi into a loading area, leave the engines running, and the aircraft would literally be stuffed with the wounded. With no loading manifest prepared, we took off with seats and stretchers full and, on some occasions, standing wounded. Every flight was overloaded and over gross weight, and the warm summer day made for a long roll and very slow climb to get above the hilltops. After a very full day, we finally finished our work and were returning home to Brady AFB for a much needed rest. About halfway through our landing roll, my right propeller went to *full flat pitch*. We were able to complete the landing roll but had to call for a maintenance tug to pull the airplane to the parking ramp. What sheer, unbelievable luck—if the propeller had failed a minute or two earlier we may not have been able to handle it.

My tour in the Far East was over but I had one more mission to fly. The day before departing Brady to return to the United States, I was scheduled to fly a trip and was assigned Lt. X as copilot. As usual, I placed him in the left seat so he could get stick time. As the day passed, it was obvious that he was well "behind the aircraft." In my opinion, he just wasn't qualified, even as a copilot, in the airplane. I thoroughly debriefed him upon our return to Brady and wrote a comprehensive flight evaluation, concluding it with the recommendation that he be assigned to fly *only* with an instructor pilot. I called the report to the attention of the squadron operations officer then proceeded to the barracks, packed, and prepared to leave for Tokyo and home the next morning. During stateside processing (a three-day drag), I received word that one of the Brady squadrons had lost an airplane in Miho, Japan Bay (the marines had a base at Miho, and our courier serviced their facility). Uh-oh…sketchy preliminary information indicated that a C-46 had "mushed" into the bay bordering the runway while executing a missed approach. Anyone with as much as one flight in an airplane knows that the flaps increase low-speed lift, allowing the plane to land at slower speeds. They also know that if the flaps are retracted before flap retraction speed, the aircraft will lose lift and may crash into the terrain over which it is flying unless airspeed is increased or flaps are again extended. I already surmised what had happened but called the squadron to confirm that Lt. X had, indeed, been crewed with one of the squadron pilots, and yes, they had missed the approach at Miho. Further, on the go-around Lt. X, acting as copilot, had retracted flaps on his own initiative (without command from the pilot). Fortunately no one was injured but "scratch" one C-46 aircraft. I suggested to the squadron operations officer that he might want to review my comments on Lt. X's flight with me two days earlier. (And here, let it be a matter of record that I did not, at any time, suggest that he might consider purloining an official air force document—especially one that would be of interest to an Air Force Accident Investigation Board).

DE PAUW UNIVERSITY AND THE STRATEGIC AIR COMMAND (SAC)

I was on my way home from Korea, I was anxious to see my family, and I wanted to get on with my next assignment. Where would it be? I had applied for flight test, but I didn't have an engineering degree, nor did I have any jet time. Chances were not good, but maybe, just maybe, I would luck out. *You bet!* So much for that dream; instead, I was headed for De Pauw University, at Greencastle, Indiana, as an assistant professor of Air Science and Tactics (a long three-year assignment). I was going to be a ground-pounder, teaching military subjects and would be attached to Bakalar AFB (a reserve base at Columbus, Indiana) flying C-46s to maintain my flying proficiency. My wife contends that the air turned blue for the next half hour.

I have but three memories of the next year and a half before I escaped and returned to flying. None of them are of any real consequence. That pretty well summarizes my view of the value of that tour to both the air force and my career development. The first is that De Pauw was loaded with tenured personnel whose uppermost concern was where they stood in the pecking order.

De Pauw University Circa 1963

The second is of an ROTC student who came to me with a question and made the mistake of sitting on my desk. The third is the memory of a B-17 in flight *with all four engines feathered* (engines stopped, propellers not turning)! To further elaborate on that memory, Bakalar AFB was located several miles south of Weir Cook Airport at Indianapolis. I had gone to Bakalar, checked out an airplane, and was in the vicinity of Indianapolis getting some flying proficiency when my partner and I spotted a B-17 in level flight at approximately four thousand feet—with all four engines feathered (all four engines stopped, propeller blades streamlined for minimum resistance to the wind). Alarmed, and naturally assuming that the aircraft was in a dangerous emergency situation, I flew closer to see if I could be of any assistance. And then I spotted it—there, mounted in the nose section, was an unfamiliar-looking engine, and it was powering the airplane. I learned later that the Allison Engine Company was using the B-17 as a test bed for their new turboprop.

SAC's Finest

Eighteen months into my AFROTC tour, SAC (Strategic Air Command) began to run short of pilots, and they issued a high-level priority levy on the air force personnel section called Blue Flame. It was designed to return pilots in ground assignments to the cockpit. Those who volunteered and were qualified would be assigned as aircraft commanders (AC) at the completion of training. *Right down my alley.* I had served my penance, and now it was back to flying. SAC was not my choice of command, but now was not the time to look a gift horse in the mouth. Selection, school assignment, and B-47 training at McConnell AFB near Wichita, Kansas, went well and surprisingly fast. Upon completion of training, I learned that I would be assigned to Schilling AFB in Salina, Kansas, and was given two weeks to check in at my new base.

My wife and I decided to return to our hometown of Spencer in northwest Iowa for a visit and a couple of days of R & R (rest and relaxation) before returning to Salina. Salina was on the road to northwest Iowa, so I decided to stop and introduce myself to my new squadron commander. All went well, but I learned, much to my chagrin, that I was going to be assigned as a copilot. This was disconcerting, to say the least, because the implementing directives were very clear that "qualified personnel" would be assigned as aircraft commanders. I had knocked around the air force long enough and trained too many pilots to really want to fly the second seat (had De Pauw's "pecking order" boorishness found a nesting place?) Maybe, but I saw it from a different angle. It was obvious that Schilling did not need aircraft commanders and wanted to promote their own. That was understandable, I really respected an organization that wanted to take care of its own. But I was no longer the new and naive kid on the block. I realized that in SAC, rank attached itself to the seat you occupied in the airplane.

Since SAC Headquarters at Offutt AFB in Omaha, Nebraska, was right on my road home, I decided to stop at the SAC Personnel Office and check to see if there might be another base that *did* need aircraft commanders. Good thinking; reasonable assumption? I thought so. I pulled into SAC Headquarters shortly after 1300 hours (1:00 p.m.) and quickly found my way to Personnel. After a short explanation, I was ushered into a L/Col's office who was the project officer for Blue Flame. I was pretty confident that my problem would be solved. I explained the Schilling situation and my own flexibility. His immediate grasp of the situation was refreshing, and I was sure that some form of remedial action was forthcoming. *Was it ever!* He immediately reached for one of the phones on his desk and said, "Let me speak to Col. B" (the Wing commander at Schilling). He quickly explained to Col. B, in very positive terms, how Blue Flame worked and, apparently, received assurance that the wing commander not only understood the program but would ensure that the attached bomb squadron commanders were thoroughly briefed. The exchange had been rather brisk, so it didn't take much imagination to realize that Col. B might be experiencing some consternation. There was no doubt in my mind as to where that might be vented. My administrative inexperience had placed me in a precarious position. I had thought that since I had not officially checked into the base, my visit to SAC Personnel was a reasonable move on my part to insure my career development. I suddenly realized that I was actually in the position of having gone over the head of my commander to try to secure a coveted position. This was absolutely verboten. I was assured of my aircraft commander slot, but I feared that there would be more to this story.

cockpit-Boeing b-47

We continued on and spent three or four days visiting with the family and thoroughly relaxing. Well, perhaps I wasn't *thoroughly* relaxing because we still had to find living quarters in Salina, and I had the nagging suspicion that my reception at squadron operations would be less cordial than when I had passed through a few days earlier. Upon returning to Salina, we found that it was a nice sleepy town with some very old but attractive houses, and many of them were for rent to personnel at the air base. After a few days of searching, we found a nice two-story that was somewhat in need of cleaning and a bit of repapering, but the price was reasonably good, so we signed a lease. I still had three days before I had to report for duty but decided to call operations to let them know I was back in town and had found a place to live. They were cordial enough and advised me that I was scheduled for my squadron AC check on the morning of my return and that crew briefing time, at the aircraft, was set for 0800 hours (8:00 a.m.). They recommended that I come out in the next day or two and pick up my flight gear and helmet. I decided to go immediately and complete that task (I was also anxious to see what my reception was going to be like). Again, everything seemed to go well. Squadron operations was rather quiet as most of the crews were out flying; my gear was issued, and I was assigned a locker by an administrative sergeant. I departed feeling a bit more at ease, but since I had not encountered any of the supervisory brass, I still had the nagging sense that the other shoe had not yet fallen.

Well, no time to worry. We had to get the house into shape, and there was a lot of work to be done. The next two days were a blur of activity, cleaning, and removing and replacing wallpaper from early morning until well into the night. My wife and I were both strong and vigorous, but we were both exhausted as we went to bed the night before my flight check. I had not taken time to review the airplane manuals because my training had gone well. I was confident in my knowledge of the airplane and emergency procedures and felt that the B-47 was fairly easy to fly. Besides, throughout my entire air force career (now going on seven years) I had always been involved in training, evaluating, and flight check. I had participated in hundreds of flight evaluations, good, bad, and indifferent; and I had seen, first hand, some of the crappy stunts occasionally employed by unprofessional check pilots. I had never needed or wanted any quarter when my own expertise was on the line, and I had *never* blown a flight check!

The Bad Start of a Crucial Day

I went to bed about 11:00 p.m., totally exhausted, and set my alarm so as to allow an hour more than I really needed to get up, dress, grab a bite to eat, and report to the flight line. Near disaster was now less than nine hours away. The alarm rang, and unbelievably, in my state of fatigue, I reached over and turned it off—but then ended up *falling back to sleep* (the one and only time in my entire life that this ever happened). About an hour and a half later I awoke, looked at the clock, and to my horror realized there was only fifty minutes before my aircraft briefing time. (SAC policy required a formal, at-attention, crew briefing at the airplane before the start of each flight.) No time for food, shower, or even a shave. I threw on my flight suit and laced those time-consuming boots, grabbed my helmet, raced for the car, and literally flew (at speeds up to ninety miles per hour) to the base. I knew there was a gate at the north end of the base—which was in close proximity to the flight line—and that would save me a few minutes. But it was not to be—*the gate was closed*. I was forced to retrace my route and go through the main gate; this cost me four or five additional minutes. Fortunately the base air police were probably on a coffee break as I made the mad dash to the squadron parking lot. I grabbed my parachute and ran to the flight line and my assigned aircraft, arriving at almost exactly 0800 hrs. My crew was already at attention under the wing of the aircraft, apparently at the direction of my assigned check pilot. I turned to introduce myself and planned a short apology to my aircrew for not having arrived sooner. As I did so, I noted the eagles on the shoulders and knew, before even looking at his nametag, that, sure enough, this would be Col. B. The next two and a half hours were an incredible flurry of events that are indelibly burned into my memory to this day. However, if the good Lord ever served as a copilot, he was there that day. The flight proceeded without a hitch, there were no repeat maneuvers, and we returned to Shilling approximately forty minutes early for an ILS (instrument landing system) approach and landing. Short flight checks could be a good omen, but was it possible that I had been set up for a preordained "unsat" (failing) conclusion?

I had long ago learned that the secret to ILS approaches was to keep the aircraft completely stable in its descent, using small power and control surface trim tab changes so precisely that you can remove your hands from the controls, and there would be no resulting change in aircraft attitude. Fortunately, this was my lucky day and the ILS went beautifully. (I hesitate to make such a comment because it sounds like utter smugness and arrogance. I've certainly had my share of bad days in the cockpit, but luckily, this was not one of them.) On our landing rollout, Col. B said, "Go ahead, taxi in and shut down." The ride was over, and I felt sure that I had passed the check, but over the years, I had seen a few "airplane drivers" receive a very brutal and rude awakening when the debriefing began. As we crawled out of the airplane Col. B motioned me over to the side of the ramp for one of the shortest debriefings of my life. He very courteously suggested that I allow a bit more time for crew briefing. Other than that, he indicated his overall satisfaction with my performance and graciously commented that the ILS approach was "one of the best I have seen." With that, he reached out to shake my hand, smiled, and said, "Welcome aboard." I had just completed one of the most memorable check rides I would ever experience, and I could not help but admire the restraint and objectivity that he demonstrated toward a young air force captain whose judgment could reasonably be viewed as questionable.

Building a Crew

Things went well for me at Schilling. I was given an additional assignment as the squadron ground training officer and ultimately received a letter of commendation for my efforts. Flying for SAC was a whole different ballgame. Crews were formed and remained together as a team. The theory was that the pilot, copilot, and bombardier/navigator would learn to function as a single, highly efficient unit. There was merit to this argument, but the other side of the coin was that the crew's progress was dependent upon the weakest link in the crew. Major G, my assigned navigator/bombardier, was a delightful guy, but the .89 Mach cruise speed of the B-47 was a bit much for him. He handled simulated (electronic target) bomb drops well, but navigation was his nemesis. One night, on one of our ninety-day deployments to Greenham Common RAF Base (just outside London), we were scheduled to proceed over water to Spain (we could not overfly any part of Spain) then turn and proceed to a point near Paris before returning to England.

Mutterings, coming from the nose section of the aircraft, began to foretell the difficulties that lay ahead. The night was clear, and as I began to make out a glow of lights on the horizon, I became a bit uncomfortable since I had not heard a word from Major G, except for two or three heading corrections. At what I estimated to be one hundred miles from the Spanish landfall, I called on the intercom to advise Major G that we were approaching Spain and reminded him that a turn *had* to be made before we overflew the coastline—actually, it should be made before we entered the Spanish coastal water. I got a "Yeah, yeah, I'll have it for you in a minute." Finally, I called again and advised that I would have to turn within *two minutes* and requested a new heading. As we headed northward, Major G kept calling for course corrections to the right. I was not exactly comfortable with this because a cloud cover had moved in below us and map following was difficult. *Finally,* the lights of Paris became identifiable through the clouds, and thankfully, they were about where they should be. We soon made our last turn and headed home to England, and now there would be a multitude of radio aids that I could use to cross-check our route. The mission ended without incident, but "lead crew status" was obviously a long way off.

It seemed that most of our missions were scheduled for a 1900 hours (7:00 p.m.) departure. On one of these missions, we were to depart from Greenham Common AB, rendezvous with a tanker over central England, take on a short load of fuel, and return home. Minutes after takeoff, I heard swearing over the intercom and Major G's painful confession that he had "forgotten" the equipment we needed to find the tanker. We decided to continue, contact the tanker, and advise them that "our equipment had failed," but that we wanted to complete the night's scheduled work. They agreed to provide us with their location relative to various English radio aids as our flights continued. Finally, we spotted the tanker on the horizon, pulled into position, and took on our fuel. I don't know if ops ever learned what really happened, but fortunately, I was never called on to debrief that mission. We completed our tour and returned to the United States to continue our training.

A Couple of Near-Misses

As June 1957 approached, our squadron discovered that we were delinquent in many of our AFR 60-8 requirements. (These were minimum, set-in-stone, crew proficiency training items; the lack of which results in an immediate downgrade from lead crew status.) It was serious stuff for the crews involved, but it meant disaster for the commander/s of the squadron/wing. The obvious solution was a mass gaggle designed to cover all the empty squares. The wing applied for blanket coordination and FAA IFR (instrument flight rules) clearances necessary

FROM CLOD BUSTER TO CLOUD CHASER

for such a large operation. Operations of this type were not unusual in SAC, but on this occasion, SAC itself had a major operation of its own underway, and it would not be able to supply the essential support, including the IFR clearances. However, there was an alternative type of clearance called "IFR VFR on top." This did not provide assigned altitude protection but allowed us to fly as long as we could maintain visual separation at our working altitudes (rather difficult in high-speed aircraft, especially when visibility is reduced but is still above the minimums for IFR VFR rules.). What was a wing commander to do? He was, essentially, damned if he did, but also damned if he didn't. The mission had to go.

We were briefed on the mission, the required accomplishments and the necessity for each aircraft commander (AC) to provide his own separation. One intrepid AC arose to ask, "Colonel, what if we can't maintain VFR?" The answer, "Captain, it is your problem, you'll have to work it out" was unbelievable. To this day, I can hardly believe that I heard that conversation. As I departed ops I was concerned, and it occurred to me that there might be several airplanes following or crossing airways without IFR clearances. As a matter of fact, I would just about have bet my life on it—and that's just what I did. I decided that I would fly five hundred feet off the altitudes we normally flew just in case I came close to another, but yet unseen, aircraft in the area. Pilots who fly at high altitudes know that when there is no visible horizon, the eyes do not always focus on where you think they are focused.

Also, closure rates at combined speeds in excess of one thousand miles per hour (approximately one mile per four seconds) make it virtually impossible to take corrective action, even if another aircraft is spotted on a collision course. The day was fairly clear, but about four hours into the mission, near the town of Waterloo, Iowa, visibility became somewhat reduced. All of a sudden, I flew into a cloud and encountered heavy turbulence—strange and unusual. Then I realized that I had flown into the slipstream and wake turbulence of another airplane that was head-on. My five-hundred-foot off-altitude decision probably prevented a midair collision. I will never know if I missed an airliner or, more probably, another B-47. Once more, extreme good luck seemed to prevail. In retrospect, I doubt that mission would escape today's tabloids. But in 1957, Korea was a recent memory, the Cold War was still intense, SAC was the nation's first line of defense, and General Curtis LeMay (Commander of SAC) was the ultimate general officer in the country.

Not all near misses occur in the air. My wife and I had taken the opportunity for a short vacation to northwest Iowa for a visit with my parents. My sister was also visiting, and she decided to spend a few days with us in Salina. During the drive home, I became fatigued and asked my sister to take the wheel for a short time while I retired to the backseat with my two older children to catch a quick nap (our youngest child was an infant, sleeping in her mother's arms in the front seat). Approximately an hour and half later, I was awakened from a very deep sleep by a shrill scream.

Sitting up abruptly, I looked over my sister's shoulder to see that we were in the left lane and about to meet another car head on. Sis, in a total panic, had simply frozen. In the right lane, I saw that there was a large semi-trailer truck, and the front of our car was abreast of the rear of the driver's cab. I had no way to gain real control of the car, but I lunged over the seat, grabbed the steering wheel, and pulled the car sharply toward the truck. In the forties and fifties, long-haul truckers were the "knights of the highway," and I hoped that this particular knight would see our dilemma and swerve to the shoulder to make room for us.

No matter what was to happen, I knew nothing could be worse than a head-on collision at sixty-five miles per hour. In the fifties and early sixties, many cars were not equipped with seat belts, and in this case, had I been wearing a belt, I would not have been able to reach the steering wheel. (Do not misunderstand me; I thoroughly endorse seat belts, but I am relating an account of an event and its outcome.) The truck did move to the right, and we did not have a head-on collision, but I had pulled the wheel so sharply that the rear of my vehicle slid to the left and impacted the left side of the oncoming vehicle. But, thankfully, we had avoided the head-on and no one was injured. As I reviewed the accident, I found my sister had been following the truck, wanted to pass, and had finally reached a point where there appeared to be no oncoming traffic. However, what appeared to be a clear stretch of highway was very deceiving. The highway actually made a curve to the right (not visible to her from behind the truck), and a county road stubbed directly into the highway, making it appear to be a continuation of the highway. The oncoming car was coming around the curve and had been hidden from view. By the time it came into view, Sis no longer had time to drop back behind the truck. Fortunately, the truck driver had seen our plight and was able to use the small change in the road bed and the shoulder of the road to give us room to squeeze through. A potential tragedy had been averted. Once more, I could not help but give thanks for our escape from a situation that was well beyond our ability to correct.

THE QUANDARY

In 1956, my father was operating a feed, seed, and commercial fertilizer business. Always interested in innovative ideas, he began to develop an idea for a commercial fertilizer spreader—something that would benefit both the farmer and his own commercial business. At that time, fertilizer spreaders were large truck-mounted machines that were loaded with fertilizer. In the field, fertilizer would be released onto a moving belt, then conveyed to the rear of the machine and dropped onto a rotating fan that would then throw it approximately ten feet to either side of the truck's centerline. However, my father's research revealed a disturbing fact about the current process—even the best of these machines were, in a sense, failures. The fertilizer materials (nitrogen, phosphate, and potash) were made into a granulated product and sold in six to eight combinations of ingredients appropriate to a particular soil's need. There were a couple of problems with this: the available combinations were never a perfect match for the farmer's needs, and in the granulating process, the tiny fertilizer pellets were not of equal size and weight. Have you ever taken a baseball and a ping-pong ball in one hand and attempted to throw them? If so, you know that they do not travel the same distance. The same principle applied to these very small fertilizer pellets, and this resulted in an uneven distribution of materials, over fertilizing part of the twenty-foot swath behind the truck while under fertilizing the remaining part. The final result was poor crop growth and less income to the farmer. Dad vowed, "By golly, if I cannot build a better machine, I will quit this business."

I began to work with Dad over the phone and on trips back home. We bounced ideas off each other, and Dad frequently made small-scale models to test the feasibility of some of our ideas. I had taken mechanical drawing during my short attendance at Parks Air College and was able to take his finalized plans and convert them into mechanical drawings suitable for blueprint production. A detailed description of the machine is too complicated but Dad had "by golly" developed a very innovative machine that allowed the farmer to (1) buy exactly what was needed and (2) have it distributed with almost perfect uniformity in the field. It would be patented as the *Multispread*. In the meantime, Dad proceeded to have a prototype made and put it into operation in his own business. The first machine was a rather awkward-looking piece of work, but it did perform as forecast. He ultimately took his plan to another manufacturer (Ranco Manufacturing), and a more refined design was developed. It was apparent that Dad's operation was going to expand rapidly, and he would require help to develop sales for this innovative piece of equipment.

Boeing B-47

Leaving Active Duty

I was not a big fan of SAC. Reflex tours (short term deployments to minimize flight time to assigned targets) were a constant interruption of family life, and the B-47 was not, in my opinion, a pilot's real dream. It had a cruise speed of .89 Mach, and at .92 Mach, the aileron was prone to overpower the very flexible wing; this created a condition known as "aileron reversal/ wing warp" (control inputs that result in airplane movements that are exactly opposite to that which is expected) creating a situation that would be sure to fray the nerves of some unsuspecting air jock. Also, in normal flight, turbulence could cause the wing to flex as much as five feet, which could be rather disconcerting to newly assigned crew members. Additionally, there were countless hours of target study, and when airborne, 90 percent of the flight time was accomplished on autopilot. I also began to observe that the real "sharp" senior captains and young majors were bailing out. My squadron commander and the wing commander had both spoken to me, suggesting that I apply for a regular commission, but I was slowly and inexorably moving toward a very painful decision—that of leaving the air force.

Dad and I had always enjoyed a great relationship. We were not *buddies* in that we didn't fish together (although we occasionally found time to hunt together), but we enjoyed working together, and it looked like there would be plenty of that if I returned home. I also knew that there was an Air Guard unit at Sioux City or Des Moines, Iowa, or maybe both. But this didn't particularly help my decision-making because I had once stopped for a refueling at an East Coast Air Guard base, and their casual, almost slovenly, appearance left a very negative impression of the Air Guard. Would the Iowa units be any more professional? My decision—to stay or to go—would be one of the most excruciating choices of my life. It was with great misgiving that I submitted my letter of resignation, which was approved by the squadron but disapproved at the wing. It was forwarded to SAC Personnel where it did receive an affirmative endorsement.

Going Home

In September of 1957, I found myself a civilian headed for northwest Iowa and what I expected to be a completely different life. I had not finished clearing the base before I began to miss the air force—even SAC. September through March was normally a quiet time in the farming community, but the farmers and local horse and pet owners always needed feed. More importantly, there was work to be done on the Multispread. Dad's store became a gathering place for friends and customers to pass the time, tell stories, and occasionally, spend a few bucks. Dad was a wonderful "people person." He loved people, enjoyed jokes, and was a good storyteller. I wasn't nearly as adept, and I had been away from the community for a long time. About four weeks after my return, I recognized one of the customers. He was from another town, and we had played basketball on opposing teams. A few minutes after his arrival, he decided it was "his turn in the barrel," and he had a joke that he was bursting at the seams to tell. It was the *most awful, crude, dumb, stupid, joke I had ever heard.* Dad was very intelligent and a refined gentleman, but he was also a warm, people-sensitive host and businessman. He laughed and slapped his thigh, and the conversation and camaraderie continued. But I had just come face to face with a stark reality—there was so way I was going to be able to handle a lifetime of this! But how would I tell Dad? The tears still begin to well up when I think about this. But, as often happens, the circumstances of life were about to point the way.

The Multispread machine was, without doubt, a gigantic leap forward in the field distribution of commercial fertilizer. It was also considerably more expensive to build than all of the other delivery machines on the market. Most of the people using and buying this type of product did not fully appreciate the importance of the distributing system. All of the fertilizer dealers understood the advantage of the blending system and the potential for enhancing sales, but they really didn't care how the farmer got the product on his fields. The trucks had always been an adjunct to sales, but very few (spell that none) fertilizer dealers were interested in supporting the farmers field application costs. As a result, there was a lot of interest (oh's and ah's) but few actual sales. Ranco Manufacturing wanted to manufacture and sell the blending system, which was essentially the truck box without the lateral distribution system. My father's primary concern had always been the delivery of a better product and more profit for the farmer. He strongly believed that the unit had to remain intact as a blending *and* a distributing system. He and Ranco Manufacturing were unable to reconcile their difference of opinion, and Ranco would ultimately proceed to build and sell the blending system (very successfully, as it became a major factor in their multimillion dollar operation). After months of discussions, Ranco steadfastly refused to pay any royalty on the machine. In the meantime, the income from Dad's feed, seed, and fertilizer business was not going to be sufficient to support the economic needs of two families.

ANOTHER MOVE

In late 1957 and early 1958, it became increasingly evident that I needed to find a job and carry my own weight. I sorely missed flying, and although there were several job possibilities, none related to flying. However, I soon went to work for Financial Industrial Fund, one of the leading mutual fund companies at that time. I had no training in the financial field, but investments in mutual funds appeared to be quite safe, and the ten-year history of the FIF funds was impressive. After a short training period at the home office, I applied for and was granted a license to sell securities. A few days in the field observing actual sales calls completed my preparation, and I was on my way to New Orleans, Louisiana, as a division supervisor for FIF Industrial Fund. My job was to sell the FIF programs and develop other sales personnel in the area. I had the strong feeling that I had just flown into a thunderstorm and every instrument in the cockpit had gone blank—and that feeling was not far afield. I quickly learned that people in the Deep South tend to hold their doctors, lawyers, and financial advisors as personal friends of long standing. I found the people to be warm, hospitable, and courteous, but slow to invest with a salesman who obviously had not spent much time south of the Mason-Dixon Line. There wasn't the slightest hint of a drawl in my voice, and I didn't pronounce the name of their cities and towns properly. Before long, I discovered that New Orleans was known as *Noo Awlins*, and my small town of "Metairie" was better known as *Metree*. In the meantime, sales and income were clearly not going to cover the cost of barebones living.

A few days after arriving in town, I learned that the air force was forming a new reserve squadron based at Alvin Callender Naval Air Station, just a few minutes south of the center of New Orleans. The next morning, I checked in with the operations officer to inquire about the possibility of available billets. After WWII and up until September of 1958, the air force policy was to assign an active duty cadre (popularly called AFTRAC) to train and monitor reserve personnel in the performance of their duties. I learned that the New Orleans reserve unit was slated to receive F-86 jet fighters (then in use in Korea); consequently, all of the assigned AFTRAC flying personnel were F-86 qualified. My heart sank. I had no jet experience, and while I had accumulated a fair amount of single-engine time, none of it had been in a first-line fighter. The operations officer was cordial, and after a few brief introductory comments, said, "Before we continue, I need to tell you that the squadron's mission has changed. It has been designated the 357th Troop Carrier Squadron [TCS], and we will be flying C-119s.

Fairchild C-119

"Do you have any multi-engine experience?" I could not believe my good fortune—and things would get even better. After a short review of my active duty career, he continued, "I don't know if you will be interested, but the air force is terminating its AFTRAC system in favor of one called Air Reserve Technician Training. Under the ART system, key personnel assigned to the reserve unit will be employed on a full-time basis to perform their functions. This program has just opened up, and I would be happy to recommend you for one of the positions." *You bet I was interested!* I didn't have the rank for squadron commander or squadron operations officer, so I filed for a job as a squadron training officer. My application was approved, and within three weeks, I was again fully employed as a pilot—the first to be employed under the air force's new Reserve Air Technician program (which, incidentally, was very similar to a program that had been used by the Air National Guard for several years).

BUILDING A SQUADRON

At Alvin Callender Naval Air Station, it was going to take several weeks before the operations officer and the squadron commander would be in place. In the meantime, I wore all the hats. The AFTRAC personnel were leaving, and I was more or less responsible for all activities pertaining to operations. A major part of this was to bring the facility up to speed. We needed desks, telephones, lockers, and all the logistical equipment that one normally takes for granted. This, along with the responsibility for the flying operations, meant that I was busier than the proverbial one-armed paper-hanger. One day, we received a shipment of lockers, but there was no one to assemble them. We still had four AFTRAC flight engineers on board, and since our reserve engineer staff had grown significantly, there was less and less work for the AFTRAC personnel. I decided to ask the four AFTRC servicemen to assemble the lockers. After a couple of hours, they came to me, strongly protesting that this was outside their job descriptions. I found this to be very frustrating, especially since everyone else in the squadron was really

busting their buns in a very congenial effort to bring
the unit up to speed.

It just so happened that I had to take a flight that
very night from New Orleans to Michigan to off-load
some cargo and return to the base. Because of the
pressure for checkouts and other training, the squadron
had spent relatively little time on standardization. I
pointed this out to the four AFTRAC servicemen, told
them all to be on board my flight, and explained that I
would cycle them through the cockpit on a two-hour
standardization upgrade. Surprisingly, during this flight,

we actually accomplished a lot of training, and while I realize that my actual motivation was questionable, the results were very beneficial and overdue. Unfortunately, not all of the men viewed the evening in the same light, and upon return to the base, they went to the AFTRAC personnel officer complaining that they had been abused. He called me to his office and threatened to have me court-martialed. He probably had a bit of a case, but we had accomplished a necessary function, and I had placed an upgrade record in each of the men's files. My position was pretty good: the men had complained that they were working outside their job description, so I gave them a job that was within their job description. We actually did need the standardization; I had worked through the entire night while they were able to have periods of rest in the cargo compartment. The case went away. Everyone was too busy to get bogged down in useless nonsense, finger-pointing and name-calling.

About two weeks later, Major K came on board as our reserve operations officer. He had failed to make a promotion cut and had been released by the Marine Corps. I found him to be a bit reserved but an excellent officer and pilot. A few weeks passed before our squadron commander, L/Col. B, arrived on the scene. He had been released from the air force because, as advisor to a Civil Air Patrol unit, he had checked out a C-45, loaded a female companion (not his wife) on board, and taken off for a weekend of R & R (rest and recuperation). This was to be a clue. L/Col. B was not the best pilot in the world and had a proclivity for "window peeking," along with some other characteristics that were detrimental to an air force officer's career. He would ultimately resign in lieu of prosecution for pumping a couple of forty-five slugs in the direction of his wife. Fortunately for her, his shooting accuracy was on a par with his military bearing and command capability.

My association with the 357th was to be one of the most pleasant experiences of my career. The 357th jokingly referred to themselves as the "Lafayette Escadrille" (an American squadron that flew for the French in WWI), but every single one of them dearly loved to fly and responded well to training. It almost seemed that they absorbed instruction by osmosis. This made my work incredibly easier, but there was still so much to do. Initial C-119 transition training was done at Wright-Patterson Air Force Base, after which we returned to the 357th for continuation training in cargo drops, minimum run takeoffs, short field landings, formation flying, instrument and night flying operations and general proficiency. Two of the AFTRAC pilots had transitioned into the C-119, so there were now three of us to do the work. One of our reservists, Capt. M, had become especially proficient. He was able to take off from work frequently, and on short notice, he was well respected by his peers, and he loved to fly—so we quickly qualified him as an instructor and relied on him heavily for assistance. Our reserve pilots were only allowed to receive pay for fifty-two days of training per year, and Capt. M quickly ran out of "pay time." In spite of that, if we ran into a bind, he was more than willing to lend a hand even though he knew we could not pay him beyond the fifty-two days. I felt deeply indebted to this fine officer and was more than happy to cut him some slack a few months later when he was promoted in his civilian work and began to have difficulty making our minimum drill requirements. He had spoken to me about this and explained that he felt the condition would work out over a period of a few weeks. I assured him there would be no problem for three or four months, and if it went beyond that we could talk about it again.

About a month later, we had been doing some night flying, and by pure happenstance, Capt. M and Lt/Col. B were still in operations as I was leaving, so I invited them to the house for a nightcap. After a couple of drinks, L/Col. B turned to Capt. M and asked him why he had been missing some drills. What was the problem? Capt. M explained the situation and went on to say that he thought he would soon be able to increase his drill activity. Lt/Col. B's comment was, "Well, you're going to have to get with it soon or we will have to let you go." He then looked at me and said, "Isn't that right, Ozzie?" I deeply resented his choice of time and place to dress down one of our very faithful and most productive crewmembers. I also felt that he was "piling on" (which, in my opinion, is a coward's way of handling what should have been a private and sober discussion). I saw the incident as one more manifestation of this officer's total lack of military bearing and command qualification. I looked directly at him and said: "Colonel, Jerry has given a lot to this unit, probably more than any other one individual, and I don't see a problem backing off for a few weeks to see how things work out for him."

Up until that point, I had always been L/Col. B's assigned instructor pilot when he went on a trip or flew the lead in one of our formation exercises. After that evening, he never flew with me again. To add insult to injury, about ten days later, I received a memorandum from him, criticizing the punctuation I had used in a piece of inter-office correspondence addressed to him. This was an innocuous error; nevertheless, the memorandum stated that a copy would be placed in my 201 (personnel) file. What was a poor (but angry) captain to do? I dug through our files, found three examples of the same type of error, and forwarded these to him with the explanation that I felt my correspondence was consistent with what I perceived as squadron policy. Would you believe that *all three of these* examples carried his signature? I had won a small skirmish, but I knew the war was just beginning…

As I mentioned above, when our aircrew personnel returned from their initial transition training at Wright-Patterson AFB, we would schedule them for night transition, troop and cargo drops, instrument flying and day and night formations. Major E had not flown since WWII. His progress went well until we got to his instrument training, and at that point, it seemed to slow perceptibly. He was visibly discouraged and appeared to lose his confidence in the aircraft. As a result, I was somewhat apprehensive to find him scheduled for night formation training, especially since he had not been able to attend any of the day formation training schedules. We completed the operations briefing, crew briefing, aircraft inspections, start, taxi, and takeoff. I decided to let him get comfortable, so I demonstrated how to join on the lead aircraft, how to execute a crossover (change position from one side of the lead to the other), and some of the visual cues he should use to hold a position relative to the lead aircraft. He appeared relaxed and anxious to take the controls, so I moved the aircraft into what I thought was a fair position for his first attempt. We had been flying in an area where we had lighting from the city lights, so we had a horizon reference and relatively good visibility. Just as Major E took the controls, our route of flight took us on a northerly heading over Lake Pontchartrain. In less than one minute, it was as if we were flying inside a sealed barrel. It was a moonless night, there was no horizon, and had we not been flying with visual reference on our lead aircraft, we would have been essentially flying on instruments. Ed moved in to a position that provided approximately five feet of wingtip clearance and flew it so perfectly that it seemed we were welded to the lead aircraft. It was a beautiful performance, and it seemed to renew his confidence. He completed his training, became a very solid pilot, and we designated him a flight commander. Therefore, I was caught totally off guard one day when he approached me, obviously distressed, and said that he was going to have to resign. After a bit of conversation, it was apparent that he had no problem with the squadron. The problem was that his wife felt that the AF Reserve was more important to him than she was, and he did not want to place his marriage in jeopardy. I agreed that a resignation appeared to be his only solution but told him that I would not process the paperwork for sixty days. It was a great feeling to see his smiling face at the next drill and to hear that when he told his wife he had resigned, she was very remorseful and insisted that he not do so.

Lt. D was one of our younger pilots. I learned that he was from Mississippi, he was studying dentistry, his parents had literally mortgaged the family home to help pay his way through school, and he was married. It was pretty apparent that he needed the AF Reserve income to stay afloat financially. These factors were obviously a heavy burden and left him with very little time to hang around and shoot the breeze with his fellow pilots, let alone participate in much more than the minimum drill attendance requirements. After the briefing on one Saturday drill morning, he came to me, saying, "Ozzie, I've got a job teaching flight training at one of the air force pilot training schools this summer, and I need an instrument certificate." I told him that I'd set him up for a couple of training flights and a check ride but was then taken aback by his next statement: "I have to have it by next Wednesday." I looked at him with some astonishment and a bit of chagrin and said, "I can set you up for a check ride Monday, but you and I both know there is no way you can pass it." But he wanted to give it a try, so I scheduled him for an instrument training flight and logged myself on as the instructor. After a couple of hours of instruction and practice, I told him to get a clearance and make an instrument approach for landing at Callender. He had been responsive to training and demonstrated excellent potential; the approach had been satisfactory, but there had been too much instruction to consider it a check ride. What to do? I debriefed the flight, and as I finished, I looked him in the eyes, told him that I was going to give him an instrument certificate, but advised him, "Don't be a fool. If you want to take your chances in actual weather and kill yourself, that is one thing, but don't take an innocent passenger or student with you." I wasn't too happy with my decision, but somehow I had confidence in his intelligence and felt that things would work out. It did. He spent the summer instructing and returned for weekend training in the fall.

A few weeks went by, and abruptly Lt. D came to me again; this time to tell me that he was going to have to quit. I suggested that we go into my office and talk about it; there had to be some deep underlying problem because I knew he needed the income to stay in school. As he talked, he confided that his wife was grossly overspending their budget, and he was going to have to quit school and take a full-time job. It was apparent that the problem was ongoing and past discussions and efforts to reach a compromise had all failed. It seemed obvious to me that the ultimate outcome for their marriage was almost a foregone conclusion. I alluded to that and, in effect, suggested that he "take command of his ship" and invite her to join the voyage or disembark if the austere quarters and frugal rations were unacceptable. She declined, and they divorced. Lt. D went on to finish dental school. He ultimately resigned from the 357th and set up a dental practice in New Orleans. Today, he is one of the leading orthodontists in the South. He is a multimillionaire and owns and flies his own twin-engine jet. We have remained staunch friends, and he periodically thanks me for "the leg up." His thanks is certainly appreciated, but I really didn't give him anything except "a chance." He is the classic example of what anyone in this wonderful country can do if he/she has the intestinal fortitude, perseverance, and courage to dream and live that dream. It isn't always easy, but the opportunity is almost always there. It may be more difficult for those that are physically or mentally handicapped, but even there, a surprising number have overcome astronomical odds to live very full and rewarding lives.

AFTER "THE BIG EASY"

I thoroughly enjoyed and respected the aircrews and maintenance personnel assigned to the 357th at Callender NAS, and I had become personal friends with many of them. At the end of approximately sixteen months, the squadron was fully manned and had attained "ready" status (fully capable of performing its assigned mission). Hard work had paid off, and we could finally pull back and relax a bit. I now had more time to reflect on the past and seriously contemplate my future. There was limited promotion potential within the squadron, and I was not interested in moving to wing headquarters at Ellington AFB, in Houston, Texas; besides, the reality was that there were no openings there either. However, the 733rd Troop Carrier Squadron (TCS) at Hill AFB in Ogden, Utah, was looking for a supervisory pilot. This would be a step up, and it paid more money. I applied for the position and was accepted.

The 733rd flew C-119G aircraft (the famed Fairchild "Flying Boxcar"). The airframe was the same as the "D" models I was flying in New Orleans, but the "G" model had completely different engines. As a result, it was necessary for me to complete a short transition course into the airplane. My assigned instructor was Major S, and I soon learned that he had also bid on the position that I now held. We seemed to get along well, and after two flights, he scheduled me for a check ride. I was somewhat surprised to find that he would be the assigned check pilot; I was even more surprised when he failed me on the check (the only flight check, military or commercial, that I failed in my entire career). I was livid. It took less than five minutes for me to "debrief"

the operations officer on the highly unprofessional conduct of an instructor pilot putting a student up for a check if he was not qualified. I also raised the obvious question: "Why did Major S feel that I was qualified one day and unqualified the next, especially since he had provided all of the instruction?" I requested that the operations officer himself take me up for a recheck without benefit of further instruction. He scheduled my recheck for the next morning; the flight was short, uneventful, and it solidified my opinion that Major S had taken a cheap shot.

Personnel of the 733rd were, again, a great group to work with. Their average experience level was more recent and considerably higher than the 357th, and many of them had flown C-119s in Japan and Korea. The year I spent with them would turn out to be pleasant and basically uneventful; however, there were a few events that I still remember. One episode concerned Mary V., our operations secretary. Her work was excellent, she was always very pleasant and professional, but she was grossly overworked and underpaid as a GS-3. She had appealed to the Civil Service Board at Hill AFB for an upgrade to a GS-4 on two occasions but had been turned down. One morning, she asked if I would help her with another appeal. We spent some time reviewing her job description, and then it occurred to us to play a bit of a game with the Board. We were sure the Board would not jump a GS-3 to a GS-5, so we decided to write the job description for a GS-4 but request a GS-5 rating. It worked. The Board's response was that although the job description did not warrant a

GS-5 rating, it did warrant a GS-4 rating. And so, this very capable and deserving secretary finally received her promotion.

Another event that I recall concerned Lt. R, who was a nephew of our squadron commander. He was a weak pilot and, for some reason, seemed to have incurred the animosity of some of the supervisory personnel in the squadron. It occurred to me that his relationship with "the boss" may have been his nemesis. I had acquired the reputation for being a tough but fair evaluator, and I found myself scheduled to give Lt. R an instrument evaluation ride. I had not flown with him before but knew him by reputation. I approached the checkout with a good bit of apprehension; I was in a tough position because I felt sure his service would be terminated if the flight did not go well. During the flight, I tried to put him at ease, but it was obvious that he was feeling a lot of pressure. He was not trimming (using trim tabs to minimize control pressures) the aircraft properly, so any diversion of his attention quickly resulted in unwanted heading, altitude, or air speed changes. We worked on that problem for a bit and then continued his check. We finally finished our work, returned to base, and I graded the flight as satisfactory. It hadn't really been *good*, but I had seen worse, and I believed that time would bring Lt. R up to speed. When I returned years later for a squadron reunion, he was still there, and he thanked me. I appreciated the thanks, but again, all I had really done was to give him a "chance," and he had done the rest.

MOVING ON

The 733rd TCS at Hill AFB was under the supervision of the 452nd TAW (Tactical Airlift Wing) at March AFB, Riverside, California, where there were three sister squadrons. In March of 1961, the 452nd advertised an opening in one of its California squadrons for the same position I currently held with the 733rd. I knew I would miss my Utah Friends but I had always wanted to live in Southern California. I also knew that if you are looking for a promotion, you need to be close to where the advancement potential exists, and common sense clearly suggested that personnel in a small outlying squadron could easily get lost in the bigger picture. I submitted my application to the 452nd, and it was accepted.

The next four and one-half years with the 452nd were relatively uneventful—except for that occasional incident that leaves its indelible mark. Flying has often been described as "countless hours of boredom interspersed with moments of sheer terror." One of those occurred one evening when we were night-flying a C-119, which had an auxiliary electric power unit

(APU) mounted on a platform at the rear of the flight deck, approximately twelve feet behind the pilot seats. We had just broken ground on takeoff when there was a flash of light behind me. Thinking that one of the students had lit a cigarette, I turned to tell him to put it out; it was then that I saw that our APU was on fire. We had already cycled the gear up, and there was very little runway left, but the fire was too large for us to continue flight. I called for the gear down, and when the gear warning lights turned green, I planted the airplane on the little bit of runway left. I immediately applied full braking and managed to get the airplane stopped approximately fifty feet short of the end of the runway. The APU fire went out as we cut switches, and the fire department was on the scene quickly. Fortunately, they managed to put out the wheel fires (caused by our heavy braking) without further damage to the airplane.

I was always alert for schooling that would enhance my personal development, so when, in the fall of 1962, I spotted an opening for a student slot at the USAF school for flight safety officers at the University of Southern California, I applied and was accepted. This would take me away from my flying duties for eight weeks, and I knew that it would result in additional duty as a flight safety officer when I returned to the wing. Nevertheless, since it would also broaden my background and overall value to the air force, I felt it was worth the effort. Little did I know that it would prove to be a job saver for me in less than eight months.

B-2   Saturday, April 21, 1962   The Press

Pilot averts air tragedy

MARCH AIR FORCE BASE —An Air Force pilot made a successful emergency landing here last night after an electrical short in the cargo compartment of his C119 troop carrier plane occurred shortly after takeoff.

Base officials said a fast-acting emergency crew doused a fire resulting from overheated brakes after the aircraft skidded to a stop.

The pilot, Capt. O. H. Hurts of the 452nd Troop Carrier Wing, cut the power and dropped the plane back to the runway from an altitude of about 50 feet at 8:30 p.m.

The crew of five and six passengers escaped uninjured from the plane and the emergency crew kept the brake fire from spreading to other parts of the plane.

The troop carrier was bound for Hamilton Air Force Base near San Francisco.

Officials said the damage to the plane was very minor and that Capt. Hurts performed an "excellent emergency landing."

My home in Riverside was approximately sixty-eight miles from the USC campus where the flight safety course was conducted. Classes started at 0800 each morning and ended at 1600. I was fascinated by the course content as it introduced me to so many subjects that I had to deal with every day but actually knew very little about. The significance of terms like metallurgy, metal fatigue, crack propagation, bending moment, and so many more had to be understood and, by the end of the course, applied to an actual accident investigation. I had a lot on my plate, and it required a great deal of homework. There was also the matter of the daily one and one-half-hour drive each way, which further reduced study time, leaving almost no room for family activity. Weekends were frequently governed by the need to catch up, and personal recreation was out of the question. In spite of the pressure, I enjoyed the school and the excellent course presentation. The eight-week course extended into the late fall and early winter with the customary potential for heavy fog in the Riverside community during the winter months. The year 1962 was no exception. I normally left Riverside about 5:30 a.m. However, one morning, I awoke to such a heavy fog that I left the house thirty minutes early. About twenty minutes west of Riverside, I was suddenly confronted with a huge obstruction across the road and, a second or two later realized that a truck had jackknifed across both lanes of traffic. I missed running under the truck by a whisker. Reading the newspaper that evening, I learned that one of the cars behind me had not been so lucky, and someone had lost their life under that truck.

Our "graduation thesis" was the investigation of an F-84 accident that had been perfectly replicated in a field owned by USC. We spent about four days looking at broken and torn metal parts, carefully noting their exact position and location along the path of the airplane. We also examined the damage to bushes and the furrowing of the soil. I was amazed to find how much can be learned from a seemingly insignificant piece of information. Even more impressive is the work of the accident team as they retrieve the parts and reposition them. It is a fascinating business, and today's progress in aviation is the result of this meticulous investigative progress and its contribution to engineering, manufacturing materials and processes, and operating procedures. Much of this work has also had a direct bearing on other facets of our everyday lives. I graduated with a certificate as a fully qualified Air Force Flight Safety Officer.

The chief of maintenance for the 452nd was a Col. M. I viewed him as an overbearing, unprofessional braggart with a penchant for using foul language in the presence of our secretaries. One night, I was scheduled to deliver a jet engine to a base on the East Coast. Col. M learned of the trip and asked if we would drop him off for a visit in a town near our route and then pick him up on the return flight. I agreed to make the stop. As we filed our clearance, I discovered that there was weather over the mountains along a direct route of flight. In addition, our load and fuel was such that if we were to have an engine failure, we would not be able to stay above the mountaintops while operating on one engine. I elected to file along a southerly route that would provide the needed safety, but it would add several minutes of flight time to Col. M's drop-off point. He demanded that I file the direct route, and when I refused he pulled his rank, took command of the flight, and filed the direct route. I could have legitimately refused to be a part of the crew under the circumstances of his filing, but decided to let discretion overcome valor and agreed to go along as copilot. About two hours into the flight, we were flying though rain and mild turbulence, and Col. M began to expound on the merits of trying to throw the (three-thousand- pound) jet engine out one of the troop doors if we should run into engine trouble. What a complete idiot! The engine would not have gone through the door to begin with, and just who was going to do that job when all of us would be engaged in managing engine failure. My comment to him was: "Good luck, Colonel. At that point, I'm going to be long gone via the nylon descent [parachute]." We completed the trip without incident, but it was obvious that our relationship was never going to be warm and fuzzy.

Several weeks later, our operations officer retired, and he was replaced (unbelievably) by Col. M. It was apparent to me that another move was not only appropriate; it was a dire necessity. In February 1963, I decided to see if the Federal Aviation Agency (FAA) had any openings. Fortunately, they had a vacancy for an air carrier operations inspector in the Los Angeles office. The job entailed the monitoring of airline line operation, record maintenance, pilot proficiency and currency, and adequacy of operating procedures and manuals. Once again, I applied and was accepted. What a relief! I returned to the 452nd to await my

March 1, 1963, starting date with the FAA. I had a better-paying job, but it was obvious that under the circumstances I had no future as an AF reserve pilot with the 452nd. Since I wanted to continue my Air Force affiliation, I checked with the California Air National Guard unit at Van Nuys, California, to see if they had any openings. Lt. Col. K, operations officer for the 146th Military Airlift Wing (MAW), conducted a very relaxed interview and explained that their pilot billets were full. *However*, they had an opening for a wing flying safety officer. Again, what unbelievable good fortune!

Back at the 452nd in Riverside, while I awaited my start with the FAA and my transfer date to the 146th at Van Nuys, I couldn't resist taking a parting shot at Col. M. At that time, the air force did not require the wearing of a uniform when on duty as a technician. It was strongly encouraged, but appropriate civilian dress was authorized. I thoroughly supported the uniform option, and Col. M was adamant about it. He held a staff briefing every Monday morning, so on my final Monday in the organization, I reported for duty in a nice suit, white shirt, and tie. He knew he was getting the raspberry, and he spent the first five minutes of his briefing ragging on one Captain Hurt.

There were many fine officers and enlisted personnel in the 452nd TCW. It also had several outstanding reserve and technician instructors; however I felt that it had a couple of serious deficiencies at the command level. Major L, one of the squadron commanders, was certainly an exception, and I am happy to report that he moved up the ladder and became commanding general of the Air Force Reserve. Col M. would ultimately be fired for hauling unauthorized cargo (his household furniture). Some time later, I was sorry to hear about the unfortunate loss of a 452nd aircrew that was trying to fly through the El Cajon pass at night under visual flight rules—a condition that did not prevail.

DESK BOUND

Working with the FAA was very interesting and rewarding—especially since everything we did in the Air Carrier Division had a direct bearing on all scheduled airline operations. Our supervising Inspector (Mr. S) was not in good health and needed help administering and supervising the various functions and actions of the office. All of the other inspectors had been on board for a considerable time, and each was assigned to a specific carrier. Because I was once again "the new kid on the block" (not because of any particular expertise), my duties soon became that of administrative assistant to the "boss." It was not my choice, but it ultimately would prove to be a major adjunct to my career. I found myself writing official responses for Mr. S as we fielded questions and complaints from the airlines, as well as the traveling public. Another major duty was that of reviewing reports of violations or infractions of air carrier rules to ascertain whether we had covered all essential elements of proof or substantiation before we passed these reports on to the regional office legal department. I may not have been in over my head, but I certainly was in up to my neck.

English literature and grammar had not been my best subjects in school, and the bit of business correspondence I had taken at night school was years behind me. Mr. V was assigned to the FAA's Regional Office (the next higher level of authority with responsibility for the eleven western states). He was a retired navy officer, an excellent administrator, and fortunately for me, he became my mentor and close friend. Almost all of our district office correspondence going forward to the regional office passed through Mr. V. For the first two or three months Mr. V would frequently call me to ask what I meant by certain wording, or he might comment, "You've already said that in this other paragraph" or "Get to the point," and all too often, he'd point out that a sentence or paragraph really didn't add to the communication and should be deleted. After several months, I began to receive occasional requests from the regional director or his assistant to prepare correspondence for their signature. They'd send a rough draft or someone would call to provide essential details and the desired thrust, and I'd prepare a draft for their approval.

The next three years passed quickly and without much incident. However, there was one rather amusing event that I often think about. One morning, one of our inspectors brought a report to me for review. The complaint had originated from a marine pilot who had observed a commercial airline off course and flying within a restricted bomb area near Blythe, Arizona. The pilot had meticulously filed his report pointing out that he had pulled up within three hundred feet of the airliner, taken its tail number, and recorded the VOR (VHF omni-directional navigation facility) range and azimuth of the incident. The report was well-written, well-documented, and the precise range and bearing from the VOR was irrefutable evidence as to the exact location of the incident. The report looked "good to go" to legal. As the inspector turned to leave, I asked him if he had actually plotted the information provided by the marine pilot on an aeronautical chart. He replied that he had not because the data seemed so precise. We decided to play it safe and draw it out on a map of the area. It took but a few minutes to realize that what we really had was a military aircraft flying an unauthorized formation on a civilian airliner in the middle of an airway. Whoops! We returned the report to the Navy (which is responsible for much of the Marine Corps administration) suggesting that they recheck our computations and "take action as appropriate." We never heard from them. I shudder to contemplate the embarrassment that the FAA would have experienced had that gotten past us because there is no doubt that airline operations personnel would have discovered the error.

Although my work was primarily administrative, I had the opportunity to participate in some of the FAA Air Carrier Division's typical day-to-day fare. Early in the second week of my tenure, the Los Angeles office received a report from an insurance company that a check issued to them by a small airline operation in Las Vegas had bounced. Simple, send it back through, right? No! If a company is running short of operating capital, you can bet that they may be taking shortcuts wherever possible to reduce costs. This invariably results in minimizing the safety of operations and increasing the potential for accident. Another inspector and I proceeded to Las Vegas to issue a "Cease and Desist" order that would close the airline down until they could mend their financial situation. In this case, they were never able to do so. We had done our job, and the traveling public was a bit safer; however, it was a traumatic event for the airline, and I couldn't help but feel empathy for the investors and a dream that was in fragments.

On another occasion, we received a report that a major politician, currently up for election, had been drunk and disorderly on a flight into Los Angeles. This sort of incident always caught a lot of publicity, and it had to be thoroughly investigated. Our investigation proved conclusively that there was no basis in fact for the report, but the damage had been done. The media was in a frenzy. When our investigation proved that the report was totally unfounded, there were far fewer reporters around. Our office had spent numerous hours chasing down witnesses and rendering the report, time that could have been used on agency business of real importance was lost—all because of a classic case of political chicanery.

One of the FAA's functions is to help new airlines set up their maintenance shops and records, ensure that their personnel are qualified, and further ensure that their airplanes are in compliance with all maintenance directives. We proceeded to Kingman, Arizona, one day to assist in a proposed new operation. When we arrived, we found the facilities minimal, the equipment old, and the operator marginally qualified at best. Our first discovery was that his airplane (an old Navy Catalina) did not meet maintenance standards. One issue was that he had decided to move the airplane's battery to a location in the wing, but had not bothered to establish new weight and balance information proving the change would not adversely affect the flight characteristics of the airplane. Another item of major significance was that one his proposed routes of flight from Los Angeles to Catalina Island ran through the middle of a navy bombing range. We spent several hours and left him with numerous pages of notes pertaining to requirements essential to his certification. Again, I couldn't help but have a great amount of empathy for the tremendous task ahead of him and what I felt was his limited ability to accomplish it. *However, this guy had a dream, and he was tenacious. He would go on to accomplish his goal in spite of rather horrendous odds.*

Work for the FAA was never dull. Every day was a new adventure. There were many amusing incidents and many with real pathos. We dealt with some wonderful people and a few renegades, and you learned never to take any situation at face value.

In October 1965, one of our lead inspectors in the Los Angeles office was selected for promotion and transfer to the FAA's Washington, DC, headquarters. There was a little discussion between us as to the possibility that I might eventually attempt to follow him. This was an interesting thought. I had great respect for him, work at the agency was always changing, and the association with a group of professionals so vital to the airline industry was rewarding. The pay was good, retirement benefits were excellent, and exposure to high level job promotion was a very attractive consideration. *However*, I was not at the controls of those wonderful machines. About this same time, I learned that United Airlines was hiring flight instructors for their new training facility in Denver, Colorado. The pay and retirement would be better, and there was the potential for eventual transfer to regular line operations. I applied for the job and was accepted. I was told later that, as of my date of hire (January 1, 1966), I was the oldest pilot to start working for United.

My responsibilities with the FAA had allowed plenty of time for participation with the 146th MAW. My duties as wing flying safety officer required a full checkout in the assigned C-97s (a four-engine transport) and all of the proficiency requirements of the assigned squadron pilots. Shortly after completing my initial checkout in the aircraft, I was scheduled as a copilot on a personnel airlift from San Francisco to a base on the East Coast. Capt. M was assigned as aircraft commander, and sergeants K and W were assigned as flight engineers. We left Van Nuys and proceeded to Travis AFB, near San Francisco, for an overnight stop, refueling, and early morning departure.

The next morning, we were well into our flight, cruising at fourteen thousand feet in a heavy overcast with lightning and mild to moderate turbulence, when one of our seventy-nine passengers came screaming into the cockpit to tell us we had a fire in our left wing. We sent Sgt. K back to assess the situation. He returned immediately, somewhat animated, and confirmed that we did have a fire—a big fire. We decided to shut down our no. 2 engine (left inboard) to see if it might be the problem. It wasn't. We knew that there was a three-inch fuel manifold that ran through that area of the wing and that the flame was burning around it. We were in a lot of trouble; we were in the clouds, there were mountains below us, and we had to get the airplane on the ground before it blew up. Our aircraft commander, Capt. M was a cool professional. He had a lot of experience in the C-97, and he also had experience flying for one of the airlines. I was the real novice on board, so I spent my time on the radios advising the ground controllers of our plight and requesting emergency vectoring and terrain clearance monitoring to the nearest area (even a road) that had four to five thousand feet of clear space. The ground controllers were magnificent and cleared us well below published minimum en route altitudes.

In our haste to get on the ground, Capt. M dropped the nose of the aircraft, leaving the power on and picking up speed. We did not realize it at the time, but a physics principle known as the "fire or combustion triangle" was about to save our lives. The formula requires heat, fuel, and oxygen in a balanced combination for a fire to start or persist. As we picked up airspeed in the descent, the fire began to trail the aircraft and finally went out because the increased airflow had exceeded the oxygen balance for this specific combustion formula. Our good fortune continued as we found ourselves only a few miles from Grand Junction, Colorado, where we proceeded for an emergency landing. The runway was actually too short for our loaded aircraft, and we also discovered another problem—the fire had burned a large hole in our left wing flap. We needed the flaps to slow us down enough to avoid overrunning the landing area—beyond which there was a sharp drop of about eight hundred feet. We decided that the hole in the flap was so large that it might create an unbalanced lift situation between the damaged left flap and the right (good) flap and thus overpower aileron (lateral) control. We also did not know if there had been structural damage to the anchor points of the actuating cylinders. Would the flaps even extend? If they did, was it possible they would fail at a critical moment? The decision was reached to make a no-flap landing and accept the increased approach and rollout speeds. Capt. M planted the airplane on the first one hundred feet of the runway, and although we were unable to stop on the runway, we were able to slow down enough to make a high-speed turn onto the taxi strip—where the airplane's weight actually broke through the macadam. Seventy-nine passengers held a prayer service at the foot of the exit stair, and I know that some of the crew had already quietly expressed their thanks.

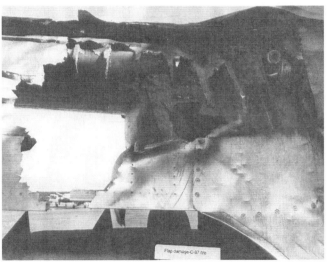

A post-flight inspection determined that in the turbulence, a heater fuel line had broken and was dumping fuel into the wing. We had received a lightning strike, and it ignited the fuel, causing a small explosion. It had to have happened almost simultaneously with the fuel line rupture because, had a large amount of fuel collected, the explosion would have certainly blown the wing off. I'm convinced that had Air Traffic Control not provided terrain monitoring, we would not have had the airspeed increase and you would not be reading this book. The newspapers played up the fire triangle solution and implied that we (the crew) had recognized the problem, applied the theory, and prevented the disaster. Let there be no mistake, Capt. M made the correct decision on our flap problem, and he flew a perfect on-speed, no-lap approach, touching down as close to the approach end of the runway as was humanly possible. It was a perfect performance. But did we apply the fire triangle resolution? Utter nonsense. I had learned of the significance of the fire triangle formula in safety school, but I certainly did not even think about it, let alone determine how we might apply it, and I doubt that anyone else in the cockpit could have even explained the theory. Later, I often recalled the crew's impressive and professional performance. I saw no fear, and I believe it was because we were too busy for panic to set in.

C-97 fire commendation

Most of our flying with the 146th MAW in the early sixties was local proficiency training, overwater navigation training, and other missions as assigned by the active Military Airlift Command in support of their role. The C-97 was an excellent transport in the days of reciprocating engine airplanes and was powered by four Pratt and Whitney 4360 engines. The aircraft was not pressurized, so most flying was done at relatively low altitudes (eight thousand to ten thousand feet above sea level). It could be a bit warm on a long Pacific haul, and since MAC was heavily involved in support of the Korean effort, and later, the war with Vietnam, most of our flights were centered on the Pacific Ocean. A typical trip was to depart Van Nuys, fly to Travis Air Force Base (near San Francisco), RON, pick up a load of cargo and move it to various locations in the Pacific— mainly Japan, Taiwan, Thailand, or the Philippines. These flights were routine for the most part and served a very useful purpose. However there always seems to be someone who goes out of his way to goof things up. On one occasion, one of our (not so smart) aircraft commanders refused to haul MAC (Military Airlift Command) cargo from Hawaii to the United States; his reason being that he did not have room for cargo. This was of interest to the MAC operations center because they had no record of any MAC cargo being loaded on the flight since it left Tokyo for return to the United States. When they investigated, they found that the aircraft was loaded with a hundred no. 5 hibachi pots. The hibachi pot was a clay brazier designed to burn charcoal. It made a super BBQ, and the no. 5 pot sold for approximately one hundred dollars in the United States. In Japan, you could purchase the no. 5 pot for five dollars, so obviously that pilot was interested in making a profit. Fortunately this sort of incident was rare, but it was unprofessional, embarrassing, and a gross abuse of the taxpayer's dollar. Regrettably, it provided some justification for the active military establishment to look a bit askance at the Air National Guard.

PARALLEL PATHS

United's training center was located at Stapleton Airport in Denver, Colorado. My family and I moved to the nearby city of Boulder and built a home on Gun Barrel Green, a new development on the northeast corner of the city. Boulder was a beautiful college town that enjoyed relatively mild weather because of its location on the Front Range (east side) of the Rocky Mountains with its typical down slope (warm and dry) winds. The schools were excellent, and it was a comfortable twenty-minute drive to work.

The training center was a beautiful facility with the best of simulators and classrooms. In 1966 FAA policy required that a trainee complete a course in the simulator and then proceed to hands-on experience and final demonstration of proficiency in the aircraft itself. I was initially assigned to the DC-6 and DC-7 programs and, a few months later, to the Boeing 727. Once again, I thoroughly enjoyed the work. My peers were exceptionally well qualified, the flight managers were low-key, and their doors were always open. One of the more attractive features of the job was that, as training center captains, we were encouraged to periodically displace a line captain on one of his regular trips so that we had practical experience in the same environment that he worked in. The only fly in the ointment was that my low seniority dictated that I was the junior man on the totem pole for choice of simulator training periods. Consequently, a large majority of the time, my "work day" ran from 5:00 p.m. to midnight. Work-wise this wasn't a large problem, but it had a significant impact on my family life. It took me away from home just as the children were getting out of school. It interfered with attendance at my son's ball games, and there were times when I was not available to help with homework. Additionally, since work schedules were not limited to a five-day week, it interfered with family weekend recreation. In the fall of 1968, I bid on a Boeing 727 1st officer position in the Los Angeles area. My bid was successful, and we sold our Boulder home and moved to Thousand Oaks, California.

Living in Boulder had made it impractical to maintain a reasonable attendance with the California Air National Guard. Fortunately, I found a flying safety officer slot with the 187th ATS Squadron at Cheyenne, Wyoming (one hundred miles north of Denver), flying C-121(constellation) aircraft. The 146th had agreed to the transfer, and I enjoyed the rather uneventful assignment and flying the "Connie," in which I accumulated approximately 350 flying hours. I have four predominate recollections of the airplane. It was the first pressurized military aircraft that I had flown. It had a very small and, I thought, cramped cockpit. When on autopilot, the tail had a somewhat odd proclivity to oscillate while the nose of the airplane remained steady. Also, loss of certain parts of the hydraulic system resulted in something called "manual control reversion," which required the strength of two pilots to fly the airplane (one would handle the yoke for pitch control and the other would handle the ailerons for bank maneuvering). I have a very vivid memory of one IFR (Instrument flight rules) approach. I was standing behind our squadron commander as he was making a low-visibility overwater approach into a base in the Philippine Islands. We broke out at about three hundred feet with a pitch angle so steep that it appeared we were below the runway level. Thankfully, he quickly recovered, and we landed without incident. Perhaps the strongest, most lasting impression I have of the 187th ATS is that of a professional organization manned by highly experienced and strongly motivated personnel at all levels. It was an honor to serve with them.

Now that I was back in California I wondered if the 146th had any openings. If so, would they entertain taking me back? My last job had been chief of standardization, 146th Air Transport Group, with the rank of major. The 187th had accepted me as a major, but many units shy away from accepting majors because they want to preserve that slot for promotion of people who have been with them for some time. Fortunately, my old wing safety officer slot was open, my application was accepted, and I was very happy to be "home." In October of 1969, I was selected as Squadron Commander of the 115th Tactical Airlift Squadron and promoted to lieutenant colonel.

This was a particularly rewarding assignment as I was working directly with aircrew personnel. Many of our pilots also worked for the airlines, and our average pilot proficiency was without peer. I hesitate to single out individuals for compliments or credit because you invariably overlook someone equally deserving. However, having said that, I feel compelled to mention Air Guard pilots Jim, Ron, Ed, Ralph, Wally, Mick, Eb, and Al who were either on board when I became squadron commander or joined the unit shortly after my tenure as commander began. Their availability, professionalism, and in a couple of cases, recent C-130 experience in Vietnam, were all critical factors in the squadron's operating success. (At this point, let me explain. When I refer to Air Guard personnel, I speak of people filling positions authorized by the unit manning document. When I speak of technicians, I speak of a guardsman who is paid to fill his/her position on a full-time basis to maintain day-to-day continuity of operations). I mentioned the pilots because, from an operational point of view, they carried the heavy load of assigned airlift missions or instructional flights that were far in excess of available assigned technician staff. Many of these missions did not require a full crew, so pilot participation might appear to predominate. I hasten to add that our navigators, flight engineers, and loadmasters were cut from the same cloth and were quick to lend support when needed. I also want to thank the wives and families of these dedicated officers and airmen for the price they paid because of frequent absences of husbands and fathers from the family scene.

Our squadron navigator, Major R, was one of the best I would ever work with. He was highly qualified, completely loyal, a consummate professional, and totally dedicated to mission accomplishment without regard to where credit might be given. I especially admired the fact that he remained aloof from an unhealthy competitive friction that I felt originated with Major J, the technician operations officer assigned to our sister squadron, the 195th TAS. It appeared to me that Major J not only tried to outshine Major S, (the technician operations officer for the 115th), but he tried to outshine his own squadron commander as well. I had no problem with healthy competition, but it seemed to me that Major J's competitive spirit was more of an undercutting process that bordered on disloyalty (at best) where it involved his squadron commander.

In April 1972, I was promoted to deputy group commander for operations, 146th Tactical Airlift Group. In actuality, there was not a lot to do at the group level. Col. P was the group commander, and he was also the technician in charge of operations. He was an excellent officer, a very good pilot, and a top-notch operations officer. He ran a tight ship and, in my opinion, was responsible for the fact that the 146th became one of the strongest, most reliable guard/reserve units in support of the air force mission. In November 1973, I was designated Group Commander, 146th Tactical Airlift Group and promoted to full colonel in October 1974. In February 1975, I was promoted to wing deputy commander for operations, 146th Tactical Airlift Wing.

I was still involved with flying, but now my primary responsibilities were largely administrative. All of my experience to date had been in flight operations and related administrative matters. I was aware of the support organizations—especially maintenance, supply, and food service—but thought of them more or less in terms of whether we had reliable aircraft to fly, adequate flying gear, and flight lunches. I had never thought much about upkeep of the grounds, hangars, offices and base security. It was time for me to come up to speed. I had a desk off the wing commander's office and went there frequently because I was determined to become a knowledgeable and active participant in my assigned duties. We had a good technician team. It would have been easy to sit back, let them do the work, and step in for the accolades when inspections went well—but there was another side to that coin. Over the years, I had observed that the technicians sometimes developed a loyalty to technician supervisors, weakening allegiance to superiors in the military chain of command. I had served both as technician and reservist and saw the problem from both sides of the fence in the Air Guard as well as the AF Reserve. It was an understandable result of the necessity to rely on experience and effort to get the job done, and it was greatly exacerbated by guardsmen or reservists who were not fully engaged in their assigned duties. I was determined not to fall into this category.

One day, while working in my office, the currency and seriousness of this problem was brought into sharp focus. The 146th ATW was a tenant at the Van Nuys airport. Its lease was about to expire, and the new lease called for a sharp increase in rent. B/Gen. B, the wing commander, called a meeting of the technicians to discuss the problem and explore alternatives, if any. He favored pursuing negotiations with the navy for tenancy on the Los Alamitos Naval Air Station located in south-central Los Angeles. Col. J, now vice commander of the 146th ATW and base commander (senior technician), had moved up over the years from his job as operations officer of the 195th ATS. He strongly favored pursuing an initial contact with the Point Magu Naval Air Station located at Oxnard,

California. Both ideas had strong pros and cons. In the case of Los Alamitos, it was somewhat centrally located relative to the concentration of reserve members living in the area. However, it was rather distant from any population density of technicians. Los Alamitos was also in an area of dense civilian population, with high surface-street and commercial air traffic congestion. Another important factor to consider was that the base facilities at Los Alamitos were in need of repair and refurbishing. Point Magu was a considerably longer drive for the guardsmen, but it was a new facility, it was a shorter drive for the technicians, and there would be less surface-street and commercial aviation congestion. The Oxnard area also presented a more favorable home- purchasing opportunity for technicians who might wish to move closer to their work. After about an hour, the meeting broke up. The door to the meeting room had been left open, and I could hear closing discussion in which B/Gen. B directed that the Los Alamitos alternative be pursued. Col. J held the technicians over and, after B/Gen. B left the room, said, "Forget that [expletive], we are going to Magu." Although I personally favored the Point Magu option, I was appalled at such raw and grossly unprofessional insubordination. Events in the months ahead would enhance and confirm the validity of my misgivings as to Col. J's loyalty, professional bearing, and conduct.

LINE OPERATION

My last flight at United's training center was as a fill-in copilot for a Los Angeles line captain on his annual simulator proficiency check. The ride did not go well. He was very nervous and had considerable difficulty with both airspeed and altitude control, and in general seemed to be a bit behind the aircraft. He ultimately passed the check, but only by the narrowest of margin. My first flight when I reached United's Los Angeles office was as first officer (copilot) for a flight on which he was assigned as captain. Expecting the worst, I was surprised to find that he flew beautifully. His command of the cockpit was relaxed, positive, and friendly. His control of the aircraft was excellent, and I thoroughly enjoyed the trip. As I was departing operations to go home, one of the flight managers called me into his office and asked how the flight had gone. I was happy to provide a very positive debriefing. It was obvious that the captain was well qualified but suffered from check-itis (excessive anxiety and nervousness while undergoing check rides).

Because of my age and late start with United, I was never able to gain enough seniority to hold a line position as captain. I flew as first officer on the Boeing 727 and the DC- 8. After reaching age sixty, I continued to fly as second officer on the DC 10 and second officer and line check manager on the Boeing 747. Most of the flights were uneventful, but two second officer checks linger in my memory. The first is of a Pan American second officer on his original qualification check with United a few days after the merger between the two airlines. The night before the check, he called me to ask what the uniform should be. I told him that the shirt and tie would be satisfactory—no need to wear the uniform coat. We met in operations, and he was very formal and appeared a bit nervous. By the time he completed his walk-around and set up the panel, I knew where the check was going. The start, taxi, and takeoff were normal, and he performed his tasks with painstaking accuracy and thoroughness. About ten minutes after gear retraction, we suddenly encountered an actual emergency situation. He handled his part of the emergency with meticulous accuracy and care. After the situation had cleared and we were again in normal flight, I leaned over, complimented him on his performance, and added, "Okay, relax and enjoy your flight. As far as I'm concerned, you've completed the check." His smile was rewarding, and there was no need for further formalities. Another check ride of note was the initial qualification of a female second officer—the first female flight officer I had thus far encountered in United's 747 program. I had no preconceived opinion concerning female flight officers, and it was gratifying to observe her confidence as well as her organization and attention to detail. The flight was uneventful, and her overall performance was above average.

I enjoyed line operations and eventually gained enough seniority so that I could successfully bid trips to destinations of my choice. London, Tokyo, Singapore, Hong Kong, and Sydney, Australia were my favorites. Carol would occasionally go with me when the flights were not full, and we enjoyed many mini-vacations over the years.

United's maintenance was outstanding, and the crews were well-qualified professionals, so work was routine and uneventful. However, there always seems to be an exception, and one trip to Sydney was an outstanding example. Pan American had used two crews to fly the thirteen-hour Los Angeles to Sydney route nonstop. United elected to add one pilot to the basic crew of three, and this resulted in the captain being away from the controls for a period of three hours at some time during the flight. Because of the trip length and fuel capacity of the Boeing 747 SP, FAA regulations precluded the filing of a nonstop flight plan from Los Angeles to Sydney. Standard practice was to file for clearance to an intermediate airport, and at some point en route—if fuel and destination and alternate weather permitted—the crew would refile, (file for a new clearance)changing the destination to Sydney. One night, the captain took his break about two hours before reaching the refile point. Head winds at altitude were greater than forecast, and we were dropping below the fuel quantity required to reach Sydney with the necessary reserve. I had been relaying this information to the first officer for the required inclusion in our en route reporting. Finally, he told me to report our planned fuel quantity rather than actual; I replied that if he wanted to lie it was his business, but I would not be a part of it. As we got to the refile point, I estimated that if we continued to Sydney, we would have less than the seventeen thousand pounds minimum landing fuel reserve required by company policy. In spite of that, the first officer elected to falsify his report and changed our landing destination to Sydney. About an hour from landing, we learned the winds off the coast were about seventy knots stronger than forecast. We also knew that at our 7:00 a.m. estimated time of arrival, it was not uncommon for ground fog to form, and this would require an instrument approach. Fortunately, it was clear when we arrived, and we were cleared for a visual approach and landing. As we shut our engines down we had just under eleven thousand pounds of fuel remaining. (A note of explanation: Jet fuel weighs approximately 6.73 lbs per gallon. Fuel consumption for the 747 at takeoff power is approximately 60,000 lbs per hour. However, since takeoff power is only applied for three to five minutes, it takes about 5,000 lbs of fuel to get off the ground, get gear up, and retract flaps. Cruising fuel consumption is roughly 21,000 to 31,000 lbs per hour, depending on weight and altitude.) Had we been forced to execute a missed approach for any reason, it still would have been enough for a very tight visual missed approach, closed pattern, and landing. I still shudder to contemplate what would have happened if a holding pattern and instrument approach had been necessary, let alone what would have happened if the aircraft that landed ahead of us had experienced an accident on the runway. Fortunately, this was my only observation of unprofessional aircrew conduct, and I look back on my twenty-seven years at United Airlines with a great deal of nostalgia.

Despite this fact, there were some situations that caused me to be greatly conflicted. In the sixties and early seventies United was the largest and best-managed airline in the world. It was not unusual to step into the cockpit at the start of a flight and find the company's president, William Patterson, sitting in the jump (extra) seat where he would remain for the remainder of the flight, disdaining the amenities of first-class accommodations. He was a very warm, friendly, humble man who was obviously concerned with employee welfare and satisfaction. It was always a pleasure to have him on board, and his relationship with the pilot group was excellent.

William Patterson was succeeded by George Keck and Richard Ferris, and the relationship began to sour. In May 1985, the pilots went on strike. I believed in, and supported, the Airline Pilot's Association (ALPA) and had served as vice-chairman of the Western Division of ALPA'S Engineering and Air Safety Division. Attendance at ALPA meetings had exposed me to what I considered the "political" side of ALPA—and it was disconcerting. It seemed that there were always a very vociferous few at the regular meetings whose only concern was to extract the last dollar from the company coffers without regard for the company's economic welfare. And it seemed to me that, under President Ferris, the company was anti-pilot at best. My personal belief was that both parties should arrive at reasonable salary scale and establish a provision for a profit-sharing program. The problem appeared to be that the company did not want to share success, and the pilot's group did not want to share the financial consequences of austere seasons. I had grown up to believe that if you accept a man's check, you are obligated to give him a day's work. When the strike came along, I was reluctant to participate. I was perturbed with both sides, so I elected to go ahead with optional surgery—something that had already been delayed for several weeks. My recovery took two weeks, and the strike was over before I got back on the flight schedule.

In 1976, I had become the first United pilot to make Flag rank (B/G and above) in any of the military services. Russ Cottel, director of United Operations in Los Angeles, arranged for a nice promotion and pinning (pinning on the rank) ceremony lunch. My wife and three children, and B/G W. (Assistant Chief of Staff for Air, California National Guard) were invited. It was a significant gesture because it helped to cement a good working relationship in an era when employers were sometimes reluctant to grant leaves of absence for military training. Over the years, I had occasionally observed reserve pilots (both AF Reserve and Air Guard) claim a military trip in order to take a day off from the airline schedule, or conversely, claim an airline trip to avoid a military assignment. I made it a point to play it absolutely straight, both as a pilot with United and as Commander of the 146th. By setting an example, I hoped to ensure that our aircrews did not abuse either party. United operations personnel appreciated the wing's cooperation, and we shared a very comfortable, friendly affiliation.

I had been troubled by an irregular heartbeat for several years, and in 1991, the problem became so severe that I had to take medication to avoid the possibility of stroke. I now found myself between the proverbial rock and a hard place. If I didn't medicate, I couldn't pass a physical, but unfortunately, the medication created the potential for sudden heart failure—so I was grounded (removed from flight status). I was never able to correct the situation and went into retirement in 1993. It had been a great job. Sadly, it has been a rocky road for the airlines since then, and many of them, Including United Airlines, have found themselves unable to make a profit. It is my opinion that the older airlines now find themselves in a particularly tough spot competitively because of high longevity, retirement commitments, and increased operating expense. As one example, during an operations briefing in 1968, we were advised that each one-cent per-gallon increase in the price of aviation fuel would cost United a million dollars per year.

MOVING UP

In late 1976, B/G B., commander of the 146th Tactical Airlift Wing at Van Nuys, California, was transferred to Sacramento, Hdqtrs California Air National Guard, as chief of staff. Col. J and I were both contenders for selection as his replacement. I was appointed to the position and promoted to brigadier general in October of 1976. I was now a flag officer. (Flag Officers are senior commissioned officers in the United States armed forces who are authorized to fly a flag that identifies their command. Normally it applies to general officers of the army, marines, and air force, and navy admirals). These officers' promotion must be approved by the US Senate.

I happened to be in my office on the day of the announcement, and when Col. J entered with tears in his eyes, I immediately felt a sense of compassion because I knew how important the promotion had been to him. A good bit of this empathy evaporated when he said, "I don't know why they selected you. You need me, I don't need you." My mind flashed back to our first meeting in 1963, a few days after joining the 146th, as flying safety officer. One of the pilots (none other than Col. J—then Major J) was practicing landings at Palmdale airport when (he claimed) the gear on the C-97 collapsed during the landing roll, and this resulted in the propellers striking the runway. He further claimed he and the crew had been able to make a miraculous recovery, execute a go-around, recycle the gear, and land, even though the inboard engine propellers had come in contact with the runway and approximately six inches had been ground off the propeller tips. I investigated the accident, and there was irrefutable evidence that the crew had forgotten to lower the gear. The wing scheduled a board of officers to investigate the accident, and I was sitting in the waiting room waiting to testify when Maj. J walked in. I assumed that he might be the pilot under investigation, so I introduced myself. Many air force pilots do not know that accidents may be investigated by an Accident Investigation Board or a board of officers or both. Inaccurate testimony before the Accident Investigation Board is immune from prosecution, but the same testimony before a board of officers could result in a prosecution for perjury. Major J. was in a bad spot, and I couldn't help but have some compassion for him. Because of this, I felt that I should warn him of the difference in the boards and the conclusive nature of my evidence. I never knew if my discussion caused him to change his testimony. I do know that he was charged with responsibility for the accident, that he was never charged with perjury, and that he never thanked me for giving him a "heads-up." However, I didn't expect one, nor did I feel he owed me one. It was understandable that he might not view me as a benefactor, but I had gone out of my way to keep him from compounding his problem. Before I brought my thoughts back to the present, I couldn't help but remember Major J's lack of loyalty to Gen. B, his competitive conflict with three of his technician peers, and his limited support of two of the 195th ATS commanders. He would continue to hold his position as vice commander of the 146th, and somehow the old adage, "Hold your friends close and your enemies even closer" began to make a lot of sense to me.

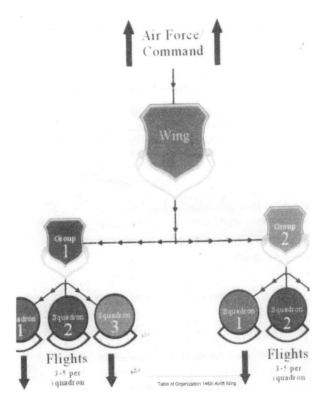

One of the first things I did in my new position was to examine the organization charts. I found that the vice commander had been placed in the line of command rather than in a box off to the side of the command line. He was also the senior technician. This gave him control over *all* of the officer effectiveness reports in the wing (excluding the wing commander), either as an originating or endorsing rater. Technically, this usurped the wing commander's rating authority except over the vice commander himself. I knew that this was an unhealthy situation because it placed an inordinate amount of power and control in the hands of one man. Much to the consternation of the vice commander, I directed that the organization charts be redrawn to reflect that subordinate commanders were responsible to the wing commander. I had seen enough over the years to know that it is imperative to clarify who is the final authority in all matters pertinent to the wing, and I was determined to be fully qualified to make those decisions. The necessity for this became apparent one day when I called a staff meeting to discuss officer development and training. I felt that too many decisions were being unilaterally made by too few people, and I was determined that problems would be staffed, and staff decisions would prevail wherever possible. After the meeting, Col. J walked into my office with the following statement: "You know, this staff [expletive] is fine, but when a decision is made, you and I will make it." He obviously still didn't get it. I informed him that I was absolutely serious about this issue and henceforth Wing policy would be that, in the event the staff's solution or recommendation appeared impractical, I would require them to rework the problem; if a unilateral decision needed to be made, I would make it.

Eighteen years in the AF Reserve and Air National Guard, both as "weekender" and technician, had given me a keen respect for the growth and professionalism that had taken place in the reserve forces. However, I felt that there was considerable room for improvement. It was common practice for the wing commander to hold a staff meeting at the start of each month's regular weekend drill meeting. These meetings often became long drawn-out sessions during which some subordinate commanders consumed a lot of time extolling the virtues of their organization—thus consuming time that would have been better spent addressing problem areas. I had seen many of these meetings run two to three hours. Add to that a coffee break and an early lunch, and 25 percent of a unit commander's time with his personnel was lost. I made it a policy that the "good stuff" would be reported in the wing newsletter for everyone to share. Wing staff meetings would be limited to one hour and were to be used for passing wing directives, policies and information to subordinate units, and discussing what could be done to help the units. I made it clear that readiness inspection failures would rest squarely on the shoulders of the unit commanders if they did not anticipate shortfalls and request assistance or guidance, if needed, from the wing.

Because of my stance concerning the responsibility that unit commanders held for the performance of their units, it was rewarding to see the commander of the 115th TAS stand up and take a very strong position in support of one of his pilots. We had run a practice ORI (Operationally Ready Inspection) on a drill weekend. In the process, we issued firearms to the crewmembers; however, we made the mistake of issuing live ammunition with the weapons (this was a drill—not an actual deployment). After the practice was over, the crews went to the club for a bit of libation. One of the pilots did not turn his weapon in at the end of the day, and sometime during the evening, he decided to go outside and fire the weapon into the air. Needless to say, this was a gross error in judgment that could have resulted in serious injury or incident. I was disturbed over the fact that we had issued live ammunition to begin with and this was compounded by the pilot's failure to turn the weapon in at the end of the exercise. The failure of supply to alert me when weapon turn-ins did not match issues was the final straw. I felt 100 percent responsible that lax procedures had allowed the incident to happen, and I needed to quickly and authoritatively address the problem. I sent word to the squadron commander suggesting that he discharge the pilot, and the next morning, he was at my office door. He readily admitted the gravity of the matter, but he also strongly objected to discharging the offender. We had a rather heated exchange, and finally I said to him, "I will make you a deal. You can keep him, but if he has another incident of any kind, he is gone, and you may as well pack your bag because you will be following him out the gate. Now, do you want to keep him?" His answer was "Yes. That is my kind of leader."

WHERE IS THE BEEF?

Two weeks after taking command of the 146th Tactical Airlift Wing at Van Nuys, I began to make it a practice to walk through the various work areas once a month—just to let personnel know that I was around and keeping an eye on day-to-day operations. On one of these walks, I was approached by an airman that I did not know. He stopped me and, after exchanging brief introductory courtesies, asked, "Do you know what is going on in the dining hall?" My response was, "I'd like to think so, but I'm guessing I am missing something." He then informed me that meat was being stolen from the food locker, so I asked him to come to my office so that we could discuss his comments in more detail. He declined, saying that there were too many people who might be watching, and then asked if I was going to attend a two-week deployment scheduled ten days later. I confirmed that I would be there. He asked me not to look him up and concluded with "I'll catch you there." He kept his word, and sometime during deployment told me that the reason the dining room was running out of food was that the mess sergeant was removing steaks from the food locker. "Theft" is a very serious accusation, and I knew it was crucial to have a full and completely reliable investigation by someone I could trust implicitly. After careful consideration, I assigned the task to Col. M. He was a WWII veteran, an excellent officer, very thorough in his work, and I knew no one was going to delude him. I was also confident that he would be discreet, thoroughly honest, and totally objective.

The results of the investigation, as reported by Col. M, were very disturbing. Sgt. T was in charge of the food service and was responsible for the dining hall menu on drill weekends. He controlled the food locker. He also ran the NCO (non-commissioned officer) club dining room and bar services. He, alone, was responsible for ordering and distributing food supplies on the base. Col. M's research validated that the dining room did, in fact, frequently run short of meat and milk before all personnel had been fed. As the investigation continued, it became evident that Sgt. T had favored friends with gifts of steaks and other cuts of meat, and may have diverted some of the dining hall supplies to the NCO club. A much more serious discovery was that there were no tapes on the NCO club cash registers, and there had been none for a considerable period of time. I immediately removed Sgt. T from all food service responsibility and replaced him with Sgt. B, who was eminently qualified. In civilian life, Sgt. B worked as an inspector for a company responsible for food service cleanliness at Norton, Edwards, George, and Mather Air Force bases, as well as the Ft. Irwin Army facility and the Andrews AFB commissary. He immediately changed locks on all food service supplies and took personal possession of the keys. He thoroughly inspected and cleaned the dining room facility and retrained food handlers. He also made inexpensive decorative improvements, creating a relaxing atmosphere that greatly improved the dining experience.

The shortage problem was solved, but we had a serious dereliction-of-duty case on our hands or perhaps something worse. I was thoroughly incensed and considered charging Sgt. T with wrongful appropriation of government property and even theft. The absence of cash register tapes was highly incriminating, but not proof of larceny. However, the more I thought about it, the more I became concerned that there might be negligence and perhaps even a contributing culpability of supervision extending from the base deputy commander (BDC) to the former wing commander himself. Where had they been? What about the supply officer? After all, he and the BDC were full-time technicians and should have exercised more oversight. I was in a quandary because there had also been several recent incidents throughout the National Guard that reflected adversely on guard management, and I was concerned that such things were becoming a major deterrent to the acceptance of reserve organizations as full-fledged members of an active air force team. Finally, and with some misgiving, I decided not to pursue criminal charges. After discussions with Col. M, I made Sgt. T's removal from dining hall responsibilities permanent and also terminated his access to the food lockers. I left him in charge of the NCO club—under very close supervision. I doubt that he ever realized what a huge break he had gotten. My actions were not out of sympathy or lack of evidence but instead were practical decisions, which I felt were compatible with all mitigating and vulnerability factors. The decisions have been a source of some consternation with me over the years, but I still believe that they were the right ones at the time and were in the best interests of the 146th Tactical Airlift Wing and the National Guard.

THE HOLLYWOOD GUARD

During the 1940s and early 1950s, the 146th Tactical Airlift Wing had an excellent relationship with the Hollywood community. Some of the movie stars of that day were members of the Guard, and a well-known 195th squadron commander, Col. P, actually became a movie director. One of our early pilots became well known after he appeared in a film that gave a lot of publicity to flying in general and glamorized the military aspect of aviation. Because of its affiliation with the stars and the free promotional aspects of film, the 146th encouraged the filming of scenes on the base itself. The base became a free set for the filmmakers at "no cost" to the wing. I was also advised (but never saw substantiated) that the filmmakers were contributing to some of the base welfare organizations. My first impression was that this was a good connection for both parties but as I looked at it more closely I began to be uncomfortable with the entire program.

The wing was furnishing personnel who provided technical advice to the filmmakers. Sgt. D loved the work. He occupied a permanent place on the set, had his own chair, and not only provided advice but scrounged incidental supplies for the set. None of this was a big deal, yet the taxpayers did pay Sgt. D's salary, and while supplies may have been incidental, their cost did come out of the taxpayer's pocket. Of course, the filming always attracted interest, and inevitably, base personnel would gather to watch. Again, the taxpayer was paying their salary and not getting full value. On one of my visits to the base, I found Col. J participating, sitting in a director's chair that even had his name on it. It occurred to me that his time would have been better spent attending to his job as base deputy commander. I finally had had enough when I observed the filming of a scene involving one of our aircraft. Apparently, the filmmakers were attempting to show an airplane flying through a storm, and to provide the effect of motion, they had people *jumping up and down on the wings of the aircraft*. Safety school had taught me about "wing loading," and although there was probably no damage being done, it was obvious that aircraft wings were never designed for this type of abuse. Ultimately, I also began to receive complaints "through the grapevine" that filming was interfering with work on the base. There were no guidelines, no policy, no apparent control, and no parameters within which the filming was being done. I seriously questioned the net benefits (if any) the wing gained from the current operation. On the other hand, it had been a part of the scene for so long I was hesitant to cancel it abruptly. But something had to be done to establish working guidelines. I instituted a policy that future cooperation would be subject to a full written disclosure that detailed the type of filming anticipated, and what support and supplies would be needed. Additionally, from that point forward, all filming activities had to be coordinated with the National Guard at both state and federal levels.

Filming was not the wing's only contact with the Hollywood community. Many stars volunteered their services to the USO and, in that capacity, sometimes came to Van Nuys. Among these were Brian Donlevy, the Three Stooges, Jeff Chandler, Charles Bronson, Tommy Lee Jones, and Lynda Carter (TV's Wonder Woman). On at least one occasion, Bob Hope and his entourage came to the base, and the 146th provided transportation to a MATS installation on the East Coast for transportation to their final destination. Most of this activity was before my time; however, I confirmed this Hollywood star activity with Sgt. J, one of the longtime members of 146th maintenance.

Sgt. J. also confirmed the history of the C-97 "comfort module." The 146th was assigned C-97 Strato Freighter aircraft—a military transport based on the B-29 bomber. Blue padded airline seats were available for installation in the C-97, but 146th aircraft were equipped with canvas troop seats to maximize seating. These seats could be folded up against the wall when not in use and quickly opened up for seating along the fuselage when needed.

Brig/Gen. C, the 146th wing commander at the time, recognized that this austere configuration was a rather sparse, uncomfortable accommodation for transportation of VIP and other dignitaries, and he expressed that view one day in a conversation with Sgt. J. Sgt. J thought about this, began to develop an idea, and then went to work on it. Why not build a module in one or more pieces which could be loaded through the large cargo door? Part of the module could contain lounge chairs, music, and a small bar. Another part could contain the galley, ovens, and beverage-heating facilities that were already installed on all of the aircraft. Sgt. J began to take measurements and then designed and drew up the plans for a two-unit installation. It would become an integrated capsule once installed and could provide comfort and privacy equal to or better than a commercial carrier. He secured the cooperation of personnel in maintenance, supply, and the base shops, and built the planned modules. When completed, they worked exactly as planned, and the wing was able to provide a very comfortable flight for celebrities, dignitaries, and VIPs. This was an outstanding example of personal ingenuity, perseverance, and dedication above and beyond that which might be expected. It represented the finest "can do" attitude often found in Air Guard personnel.

The expression "Hollywood Guard" was a problem for me because I felt that the active establishment might develop an image of an unprofessional organization. In the seventies, there was strong competition between the air force and the reserve forces, and we could not afford anything that would, in any way, foster disrespect for the Air Guard and/or Air Force Reserve. My feeling about the problematic term was validated one evening years later when Carol and I had the Air Force Air

Warfare Center commander and his wife for dinner at our home. The commander was explicit in his feelings that the reserve forces were a critical factor in the air force's total capability, and he was complimentary of the 146th's excellent reputation. However, he also commented that when he first heard the term "Hollywood Guard," it did initially engender a rather disparaging view of the unit.

DEVELOPING LEADERSHIP

In my opinion, the 146th Tactical Airlift Wing was one of the best performers in the nation in terms of supporting the air force mission. The wing was always able to turn out crews for assigned missions, and the airplanes and equipment were always ready to go. The 146th aircraft and crews were a major element in the MAAFS (fire fighting) program, and our personnel also performed exceptionally well in joint exercises. However, it seemed to me that upward momentum and the road to promotion were not well defined. Approximately one week after taking command of the wing, one of the senior maintenance NCOs approached me to complain that the rank authorized for his job was being transferred to another job on the base. I didn't understand how that could happen because each person in the military is there because he is filling a position that has a rank authorization appropriate to the responsibility inherent with the job. As a result, there is maximum number of each rank authorized for the wing, and once that maximum is reached, there can be no promotions to that grade unless someone retires or transfers, and thus creates a vacancy. However, if a particular grade is authorized (i.e., in this case, in maintenance), but it is currently filled by someone of lesser rank, the wing's table of organization would be reporting that rank as available. Normally, the position remains open until someone moves up through related work experience and seniority and qualifies for promotion into the open slot. In this instance, I found that the rank authorization was being transferred to a supply position in order to promote a specific individual in supply. I understood and was sympathetic with the effort to advance a deserving airman in supply, but the practice created confusion and an atmosphere of politics that was detrimental to general morale. In this case the complaining NCO had trained, studied, and planned his work, hoping some day to move into the higher position. Just as he was moving into range for promotion, the slot was suddenly moved away from him. I stopped the transfer and established a policy that terminated this practice. The decision had nothing to do with personalities; it was all about fairness and promotion stability.

The flying squadron also had promotional problems, but they were a bit different in nature. Many of the assigned pilots had been in the organization for years. A fairly large number of them did not aspire to move up to command positions but preferred to stay in the squadron and "just fly airplanes." This built an excellent pool of crew members from which we could draw to fill mission requirements. However, it also built a pool of high-ranking flying officers that left little or no room for promotion of our younger pilots; it was also obvious that, for example, we could not have an entire squadron of lieutenant colonels!

Another problem was that senior officers would move into and hold mid-level supervisory positions for years. I saw that this also led to unhealthy cliques, stagnation, and a political atmosphere that infected every command level up to and including Hdqtrs California National Guard (both Air and Army). I began to develop a plan that would accommodate those officers who only wished to fly. I believed that we could promote them through major, and possibly lieutenant colonel, with the expectation that they could serve twenty years before being forced into retirement. Those officers who would be willing to serve in supervisory and command positions could be placed in a developmental program of schools, duty assignments, and special details designed to prepare them for ultimate assignment as a commanding general in the guard. They would also have to realize that there was going to be a limit to the number of years they could hold a specific supervisory/command position. I reasoned that these assignments should not exceed three years—preferably two. I expected that the plan would meet with heavy resistance in some quarters because it would be seen as a threat to the status quo, but I was absolutely convinced it would make for a much stronger National Guard organization.

Throughout the years, I had seen philosophies regarding technician promotions rise and fall in both the AF Reserve and the Air National Guard. Some argued that only technicians should occupy command slots. The opposing argument was that it tied up the position too long, and the senior commander selection should always come from the "weekenders." I disagreed with both philosophies and was convinced that, with careful planning, a qualified technician could aspire to wing command, but his term would also be limited to three years. At the end of that time, he would be forced to retire unless he was selected for promotion to a position at the state level. The air force, at that time, required wing commanders to be pilot qualified. In my past experience, some of the best operations and administrative officers were navigators, and so I was adamant in my belief that this was not only unfair, but it weakened command selection and diluted the strength of the leadership pool. I decided to petition the air force for a change in policy.

It was going to take a good bit of study and some number crunching to convert my basic concept into a viable plan. Procrastination is the absolute nemesis of many a good idea, so I decided to move quickly ahead. Col. T was a logical choice to succeed me, so I told him I wanted him to take over the Combat Support Group for a bit. My plan was to protect his flying billet in every respect, but I wanted him to learn what the organization did and to have experience dealing with non-flying personnel. He accepted the assignment begrudgingly, and I'm sure that he thought I was actually trying to get rid of him. He ultimately did succeed me, but I doubt that he ever believed my motives were absolutely sincere. This was disappointing since I considered him a personal friend.

Meanwhile, Col. J was becoming a headache. I began receiving small clues and rumblings that he was not only personally disloyal, but that he was actually creating an opposition force within the wing headquarters and technician personnel. Was I becoming paranoid? After much thought and some discussion with a couple of loyal technicians, it appeared that the problem was real and had to be confronted. My first inclination has always been to meet a problem head-on, but as I looked back over Col. J's history, I became convinced that talk was not going to solve the matter. He had never demonstrated any interest in cooperating or compromising with anyone. On the contrary, he had revealed a willingness to pursue his goals by whatever means it took without regard for integrity or candidness. I did not think that firing him was an option. There was not enough of an established record to substantiate firing, and I really did not want to see that happen because he had a family, and they would certainly suffer. I also felt that the guard system itself had, over the years, created the problem.

Once more, providence played a major roll. The deputy adjutant general for the State of California was leaving his position. His chosen successor, a base commander (same position as Col. J) from Fresno, California, was refusing to leave his slot. There was a big donnybrook going on, and finally, Col. J's name was mentioned as an alternate selection. I was approached by the assistant adjutant general for air and asked for my opinion on Col. J's possible nomination; I concurred wholeheartedly for several reasons: 1) It would get him off the base and break up what I believed to be a clique that was detrimental to the Wing's welfare; 2) it would allow the advancement of Col. P to the vacated position of base deputy commander (BDC) at Van Nuys; 3) it would give Col. J a chance to prove himself in a new environment. If he didn't, I had no doubt that state headquarters would find a quick solution to the problem. Col. J was selected for the move, and Col. P transferred from operations to become the 146th BDC. As a part of the transition, Col. P elected to take his long time-secretary with him to the new position. As a BDC, it was his choice to make, and I fully understood the importance and wisdom of having a completely trustworthy person in that crucial position. I was looking forward to working with him. He was a strong, knowledgeable, competent, loyal leader, and he was now moved into contention for a future nomination to Commander, 146th Tactical Airlift Wing.

About a week later, I returned from an airline trip and found that there had been a phone call from Col. P. When I returned his call, he advised me that Col. J had passed through the base during my absence and had gone to his office to order him to send his secretary back to her old position in operations. I was incensed at this gross interference—Col J. no longer had any authority on the base. The move had not involved a pay increase for the secretary, but it was a prestigious promotion as she now worked for the senior technician on the base. I had no idea what prompted Col. J's arrogant interference—he had never discussed any of this with me. I told Col. P to disregard the order, and I would take care of the problem. I promptly called Col. J and rather vociferously told him that he was out of order, I was in command of the base, and I would not tolerate outside interference. If he didn't like it, he could pursue the matter through official channels.

After Col. J left for his new assignment, I wrote the required officer effectiveness report. I considered him a satisfactory pilot and highly qualified in his knowledge of air force procedure and administration. I commented that he demonstrated high initiative and reasonable dependability as to his personal liability and responsibility. I questioned his cooperation and loyalty in areas in which he didn't agree and suggested that further growth and leadership potential should be contingent upon demonstrated improvement in this critical area. I spent a great deal of time and effort to ensure that the rating was meticulously fair and accurate, and finally submitted it with a clear conscience.

A short time later, I learned that Brig/Gen. B was leaving his position as chief of staff for air, California National Guard, and that I was under consideration to replace him. In the spring of 1977, I received a call confirming that I had been selected for the position. However, there were storm clouds on the horizon. The adjutant general was requesting that I change Col. J's OER so that he was more promotable. I advised that I would review the report, and after review made a few minor changes in wording that I felt would soften but not change the validity of my evaluation. I was then approached by an intermediary who asked that I actually *change* my evaluation. I was also advised that when I assumed my position as chief of the air staff I would have rating authority over Col. J and full authority to rate him as I then saw him. This was a complete violation of air force procedure. I pointed this out and reminded the individual that the adjutant general had the authority and final rating responsibility in his endorsement to make any recommendations he felt warranted. I also pointed out that if I changed my rating, it would come across as if I had lied in my original evaluation. I then received a call from the assistant chief of staff for air who commented that he needed my help in Sacramento and asked if there was any slack anywhere in the report. I told him that I sincerely wished to cooperate, but any further change would compromise my integrity, and I was not willing to do that.

In the meantime, other interesting things were happening. One day, about fifteen minutes after arriving at my office on the base, I received a call from a friend at Hdqtrs California Air National guard, who said, "I hear you are on the base." I confirmed that I was and asked him just how he knew. His reply was, "Be careful, your every move is being reported." What an unbelievable keystone-cop waste of time! I could hardly believe what I was hearing, but I knew it was true because I had also learned of another recent intrusion into my personal life that was solely designed to cause a major problem with my airline employment. That intrusion had originated at the California Air National Guard headquarters. Someone was trying to dig up some dirt, and I knew where they planned to dump it. But they weren't going to find any—I had always been pretty "straight arrow" in all matters of integrity and professionalism, especially as related to the flying business—both military and commercial, and it was paying off. My mind began to grapple with a very jaded opinion of some of the people I would be working with when I moved up to chief of the air staff. I desperately hoped that the group would be limited to Col. J and his entourage of two or three people. However, I was concerned because I wondered how this juvenile activity could be taking place without word being leaked to the adjutant general. If so, was it possible that the AG had become complicit in it?

In June of 1977, I received a clue that would be definitive, and it would clarify my thinking and resolution. I had gone to Washington, DC, to attend an Air National Guard meeting. After the meeting was over, I was sitting with Col. J and Brig/Gen. W (the California Assistant Chief of Staff for Air), when Col. J turned to me, saying, "Incidentally, when you come to Sacramento you will not be writing my OER." My response was, "Okay, I guess the question is…who will be writing mine?" He answered, "I will be your rater."

I had just run into a very big career "fork in the road." The chief of the air staff normally reports directly to the adjutant general. It was obvious that the California chain of command was being politically altered to place me under Brig/Gen. J, the assistant adjutant general.

National Guard State Organization

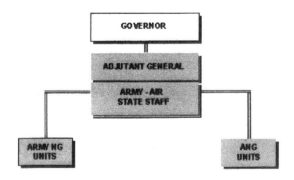

I felt that there was a lot of work to be done and the position had the potential for promotion to major general. It would be challenging, and I was anxious to get started. It was also my belief that the California Air Guard was becoming a preeminent organization in the Air National Guard which, in turn, was becoming a major partner with the US Air Force and its mission. I was also of the opinion that the 146th Airlift Wing was one of the best in the Air Guard inventory. If so, this opened up additional rungs on the promotional ladder which could reasonably lead to headquarters, US Air National Guard. But there were red flags all over the place: 1) the broken promise that I would be rating Brig./Gen. J; 2) the alteration of an official document (organization chart) placing the chief of the air staff under the assistant AG; 3) the attempt to make a change in an official document (the effectiveness rating); 4) the unauthorized "snooping" into my personal life— i.e., tracking my visits to the base and the probing at United Airlines (this came from an individual at state headquarters and did *not* take the form of a normal security check); 5) the childish banishment from invitations to functions at the base.

A hasty mental evaluation of the organization and personnel I would be working with at state headquarters (as it now appeared to be structured) presented a disturbing reality. It was evident to me that a management clique and "good old boy concept" had become a predominate reality on the "air" side of the headquarters. It was also clear that the office was permeated with politics, and I absolutely wanted no part of it.

I rather vigorously informed Brig/Gen. J that I had been in the Reserve and Guard system too long and worked with too many professionals with whom I enjoyed mutual respect to become involved with an unprofessional, inept group of clowns. I made it very clear that it would be a cold day in hell before I would associate myself with the incompetent political leadership that appeared to currently dominate at state headquarters. I then walked out. My only regret is that I did not have the opportunity to work with B/G W and develop the career advancement program that I felt the California Air Guard so sorely needed. Looking back, and from a personal point of view, I still believe that it was the right move to make.

Having once served with the Air Force Reserve, I still receive invitations to attend their general officer briefings. At a briefing in 2011, I was surprised to learn that the Reserve was instituting a program of career development very similar to that which I had envisioned—with the exception that in their program nominees for wing commander positions are limited to Air Reserve technicians. I've also had an opportunity to speak to some Air Force Reserve technicians, and they voiced the opinion that this policy works well up to the point of wing command. At that level, it has the potential to create long tenure, cliques and stagnation. Several of them expressed their preference for a two-year wing commander tenure with an absolute maximum of three (I heartily concur). The AF Reserve has the option of transferring personnel laterally to any of their many units. If they use that option, they can keep a strong commander in their system. This is a big advantage because it permits the retention of an exceptional commander through the medium of reassignment and the transfer of "new blood" into an organization that is not performing well.

THE REST OF THE STORY

I was through with the Air Guard, but I had not heard the last of Col (now B/G) J. It was about three weeks later when I received notice that he was suing me in a civilian court for $15 million for defamation of character—a result of my official comments in his Officer Effectiveness Report (OER). How could this be? It was an official and privileged document, ordained by air force regulations, and it specifically required me to evaluate the performance of personnel under my command. Well, no problem (I thought), I'll take it to the Judge Advocate General for the California National Guard who would defend me in the performance of my official duties. Guess again. The JAG was, in fact, advising Col J. (Was it just a coincidence that the JAG had been at Van Nuys, had followed Col J to Sacramento and had been promoted?) Again, no problem, I would contact the air force. The air force, in its innate wisdom, advised that it was a California Air Guard problem and they wanted no part of it. Things were looking a bit grim. It was a huge sum of money, and the cost of defending myself with a private attorney would be a significant financial hit. In the meantime, Col J (now B/G) wouldn't be out a dime because he was using the State's top military legal officer to pursue his personal claim (or should I say vendetta?). This is yet another example of the managerial dereliction at the state headquarters. In my thirty years of AF service I never saw nor heard of a single case in which the author of an effectiveness rating was sued to (1) force alteration of or (2) permit a remuneration claim against the author of an OER. Air force regulations provide for a written appeal to the next higher rating authority, but there is no provision for relief through the court system. And there certainly is no authority which would permit B/G J to use a military asset (the Judge Advocate General) to pursue a civil complaint.

Again, providence was to pull me out of the hole. About six months before this action, I saw that finances were moving along pretty well, and I decided that it would be wise to protect my assets. Consequently (and fortunately), I took out an income protection policy with my insurance company, USAA. It was a good policy that fully protected from this type of predator. There were hours of attorney preparation, a trip to San Francisco for a deposition, hours of consultation and court preparation—and then a hearing. Finally, the court issued a ruling that dismissed all charges. My total out-of-pocket expense was one tank of gasoline. While all of this was going on, I found that I was persona non grata at Van Nuys, and I was removed from all invitation lists to include both casual and official functions. Someone at state headquarters was spending so much time trying to knee me in the groin that I wondered how he even had time to attend to his taxpayer-funded duties.

I wasn't the only one on the "hit" list. Information was being relayed to me by a general officer of impeccable integrity on the staff at Hdqtrs California National Guard. According to my source, the adjutant general was following the progress of the commander of one of the units in the Hayward, California area. When that officer didn't make the promotion list, the AG called Col J (now Brig/Gen.) and asked him to investigate the matter and report back to him. Brig/Gen J. reported that he could find nothing amiss—apparently the selection board had simply declined to approve the officer's promotion to Brig/Gen. Not satisfied, the AG decided to personally visit the Pentagon and review the officers record and selection board action. What he found would finally end Brig/Gen. J's efforts to stifle competition. Brig/Gen. J had personally intervened to torpedo the Hayward officer. (Could it be that he saw him as a competitor at State headquarters?) The AG returned to his office, called Brig/Gen. J in, then ordered him out of the office and told him to never return. His career of deceit, innuendo, politics, and vicious infighting was over. He was exposed for the Judas he was. A few months later, he went on a solo scuba dive with partially filled tanks, got caught in kelp, and ran out of air before he could free himself. He had only one choice, jettison the tanks and surface. It was his last dive.

Months later I ran into the new AG at a change-of-command ceremony. He told me, and I quote, "I wish to God we had listened to you."

A BRIEF RETURN
TO FARMING

My wife and I had been married for thirty-one years. She was an excellent mother and a good partner, but my continual absence was taking its toll. We sought counseling, but we were unable to resolve our differences and we divorced. Fortunately, we have remained friends. Both of us have remarried, and we see each other three to four times a year at family functions.

I had started dating Carol and we ultimately married and bought my partner's interest in a fruit grove in the Bonsall, California area. We started a building program to convert a rundown shack into a comfortable home. There was a lot to do. The property contained thirteen acres of oranges. When the fruit was ready for harvest, I contracted with a local company to do the picking, hauling, and processing. It was a bountiful harvest, and the fruit was beautiful. You can imagine my surprise when I received a bill from the packing company for $2,500. I called the company and suggested that they may have made a mistake. Not so! As it turned out, the picking, hauling, and processing costs were more than the fruit was worth. After some discussion with farm advisors and the packing plant, it seemed advisable to remove the orange trees and replace them with avocado trees. Carol pitched in to help, and between the two of us, we cut 1,300 orange trees into firewood, got rid of the brush, and replaced all of this with Haas avocado trees. At the same time, I was carrying a full flight schedule with United, driving 107 miles each way to work, and renovating the house as well. It was already a full plate, but since I knew my propensity for burying myself in work, I agreed to learn something that was new and fun—square dancing. Carol and I then spent many enjoyable evenings doing "circle lefts and rights and swing your partner."

We continued to renovate the house and convert the grove to a profitable operation. It was a frustrating task. The irrigation system had to be entirely rebuilt, and the ever-increasing cost of herbicides, pesticides, water, and harvesting continually outpaced the price paid for fruit, and our replanting process left very little fruit for sale anyway. However, the property was shaping up. Our house plan had been well thought out, and the irrigation system had been redesigned so that fertilization was done through the watering system. It was a more efficient delivery of plant growth nutrients, and the new trees had grown well and were beginning to bear some beautiful fruit. We had also cleared trees from around the house so that there was now a clear view to the horizon. However, things were about to change again. Our neighbor was a full-time farmer who had taken a liking to our acreage and wanted a home for his hired help. In November of 1985, he "made us an offer we couldn't refuse." We sold the grove and prepared to move to Thousand Oaks, California.

I was becoming very proficient at loading moving trucks and could pack every inch of a moving van, drive it any distance over any kind of road and get to a destination without a scratch or broken piece of furniture or glass. Our friends were becoming equally adept. Three days and two twenty-six-foot vans later, the move was over.

It was a relief to be free of the financially unproductive grind the grove had become. Carol and I had both previously lived in the Newbury Park and Thousand Oaks area, and it was nice to be back in our old stomping grounds and nearer friends and relatives. We also had more time to exercise the "space available" travel provision of my United Airlines retirement (travel in unfilled seats, at nominal expense, allocated to employees/retirees on a seniority basis). The next four years passed swiftly, but freeway congestion and population density was much greater than either one of us remembered. It was becoming a major irritation we could not avoid no matter where we might be going. We had friends who lived in Sun Lakes, a nice retirement community in Banning, California, and they were ecstatic about its many advantages over living in the Los Angeles extended area. We decided to take a look and found the community to be all that they claimed. The Sun Lakes community was well designed, and there was relatively little local traffic—although there was a major freeway (US 10) within a short distance, so it took only minutes to be on our way in any direction. I was not a golfer, but we decided to buy a home with an east-facing patio that backed up to one of the fairways.

And so, we moved again—and, as usual, did the moving ourselves. We thoroughly enjoyed the new home, the beautiful view, and the quiet solitude. However, I was becoming very concerned with taxes and politics and was quite pessimistic about any improvement under the liberal climate that predominated in California. Additionally, I was still working and began to feel that I had little in common with a community of retirees. I was also missing my association with my air force buddies.

In late 1990, we took a trip to Death Valley, and on the way home, stopped to visit Carol's cousin in Las Vegas. While we were there, the cousin drove us around the city to show how it was growing and also pointed out some of the excellent real estate buys. We were impressed. There were many charming homes in beautiful locations. The prices were excellent and property and income taxes were much better than California's. And you could drive clear across the city in any direction on excellent freeways in twenty minutes. In addition, Nellis Air Force Base offered a reunion with air force friends and family; it also had all the facilities a large military installation can offer to a retiree. I was still employed by United Airlines but was grounded because of a heart arrhythmia. This made the medical facilities at the base a large plus.

DESTINATION SIN CITY AND BEYOND

Before leaving Las Vegas on that fateful trip early in 1990, we put an offer in on a home on Sunrise Mountain overlooking Nellis AFB and the city itself. Our offer was accepted, and the moving process began anew. Another two trucks, another three days, and we were in. I must comment here that if I ever start a moving company, Carol is going to be my first employee.

Things moved swiftly for us. I checked in with the Air Warfare Center to pay my respects to the commander. We joined the Officer's Club, and I joined the Daedalians (the National Fraternity of Military Pilots). We made some wonderful friends, among them Col. G and his wife Mary. Col. G was a very gregarious person and was instrumental in introducing me to the Red River Valley Fighter Pilots Association (River Rats) and the QBs (Quiet Birds, another pilot association). I'm not much of a "joiner," but they were a great bunch of warriors and patriots. I knew the "Rats" by reputation for their outstanding work in Vietnam, and I felt especially humbled to have the opportunity to join such an august group. Not long after joining the Daedalians, we invited them all to the house for a potluck dinner. This gave the wives a chance to join in the fellow/(girl)ship. The Rats and Daedalians have numerous gatherings each year and this has made for many warm friendships.

The commander of the Air Warfare Center made it a practice to invite retired personnel living in the area to most of the official functions on the base, and he also provided flag officers with an annual briefing. I was especially delighted; it gave me a sense of still being active in air force affairs and current national and international events. There were also many retired officers who had held high-level positions in the air force, and over time, I learned a lot about its workings that I previously had not known.

In 1987, B/G B, Col. M, and C/Msgt S got together and founded the 146th Alumni Association. Its purpose was to assist the active wing and its personnel in any way possible, and to provide a vehicle through which active and retired members could renew and perpetuate old friendships. I viewed it as a unique, altruistic concept, and my wife and I joined. The association met twice each year for three days. The first evening was devoted to registration and visiting, and the following morning was dedicated to a business meeting. The rest of the time was spent sightseeing and visiting. I especially liked the fact that the wives could be full-fledged participants and meet people they had probably heard of but did not know. In 1997, my wife and I agreed to co-chair the organization. I was happy to do so as it gave me an opportunity to "pay back" the members for the outstanding support they had given the wing while I was commander. One of the vehicles we used was the newsletter.

Carol and C/MSgt S were close friends, and he was an icon. He had been in the 146th for years and had been assigned to the pay section so he knew almost everyone in the wing on a personal basis. They would write to him frequently, and he would forward appropriate communications to Carol for newsletter publishing. My firm belief was that members of the association wanted to hear from their peers rather than reading something that I might originate, so with permission from the authors, we printed the letters exactly as written in the monthly newsletter. This consumed a lot of time, but I felt it was a critical element in holding the association together. Setting up, conducting, and cleaning for two reunions per year was rather laborious, but again, it was our opportunity to serve those who had served the wing so well. Our efforts were well received, and Carol and I occupied the chair for six years. My belief that military management goes stale with long office tenure also applied to our chairmanship of the association, so we declined to be reelected in 2003. There were no volunteers, so B/G B (one of the founders) stepped back into the breach and served as chairman for one year. He too felt the organization needed new blood and also declined to be reelected. He was relieved by Col. B, who was then followed by Brig./Gen. P. Brig/Gen. P put together a three-person team that has done an outstanding job of improving the esthetic quality of the newsletter, developing a scholarship program, and providing speakers at the general meetings.

In 2005, having tired of the Las Vegas scene and wanting to be near family, we moved to Prescott, Arizona. It is a beautiful area. We both became involved with the Court Appointed Special Advocates (CASA) program that is designed to protect children from abuse or abandonment. Arizona runs a great program, and Carol was exceptionally good at CASA responsibilities. She could sit for five minutes with a child and know all there was to know about that child. And the kids loved to sit and talk with "Grandma." I jokingly maintain that my CASA work consisted of providing logistics for Carol.

Because of its five-thousand-foot-plus elevation, Prescott temperatures usually ran about twelve to fifteen degrees cooler than Phoenix. Fortunately, it also did not get the heavy snows so prevalent in Flagstaff (which is at seven thousand feet). In the summer and early fall, Prescott was subject to heavy monsoons, and from our patio, we would often watch the beauty of heavy electrical storms without receiving the blinding rain and flooding that was characteristic of other parts of the city. But Prescott had a major drawback for me. The area was heavily populated with juniper bushes. I struggled with allergy medication, but my eyes would swell shut, and the itching was almost unbearable. I went to an allergy specialist, and my tests were literally off-scale-severe. At the start of 2011, we began to explore the possibility of moving.

Where should we go? Because of family connections, Southern California was an obvious possibility in spite of some rather prominent negatives. Carol began to search the Internet and discovered an interesting home for sale in the Sun Lakes community located in Banning, California. When she showed it to me and commented that it looked familiar, we suddenly realized that it was a home that we had purchased new in 1990—in fact, we had worked on the landscaping and addition of patios and patio overhangs. We contacted the listing realtor and made arrangements to travel to Banning and see what condition the place was in. We discovered that it had been vacant for four years and had some problems, but they were not serious and the asking price was basically fair. The community had grown tremendously in the twenty years that we had been gone. There was a large shopping center across the street from the main gate, and also a medical center across the street from another gate. We made an offer that was ultimately accepted, and we moved in April 1, 2011. We have seen more family and friends in eighteen months than we did in five years while living in Prescott. Carol has become involved in the care of problem children and has joined a dance group. We still return to Las Vegas to visit our old friends at Daedalian and River Rat functions, and we occasionally drive back to Prescott to visit friends and family there.

AN APPRAISAL

Looking back over my life and attempting to focus on incidents and events in order to accurately bring them to life on these pages has evoked a lot of nostalgia and many warm, pleasant memories. I am especially pleased to note the growth that has taken place in the reserve forces—both Air Guard and AF Reserve. It was a long and sometimes rocky road. I cannot forget the first guardsman I ever saw, dressed in a worn-out faded set of pinks and greens (light, almost beige, trousers and forest green shirt) worn by WWII army aviators. Col. B, squadron commander of the 357th, Col. M, maintenance officer of the 452nd, and Col. J would not survive in today's reserve system. These aberrations were part of a maturing process and have almost disappeared as management has grown.

In the 1970s, the Air Force began to integrate crews and equipment of Air Guard, AF Reserve, and active duty personnel for more efficient utilization of assets. Under this plan, it was possible that a mixture of active duty and reserve personnel flying an active duty or reserve airplane would be assigned to a mission with an active duty or reserve officer in command. The intent was to provide the taxpayer the best buy for the buck. It allows the air force to maintain a smaller active establishment for day-to-day operations because it can be augmented by a huge reservoir of crews and equipment fully qualified and ready to go within twenty-four hours. AF Reserve forces were heavily involved in both Gulf wars and are currently a major factor in the war in Afghanistan. A recent report indicates the Air Guard is currently providing approximately 50 percent of the air force's tactical airlift support. These forces participate in combat communications, aero-med evacuation, aerial refueling, fire fighting, and are responsible for aerial defense of the United States as well. The same report indicates that the Air Force Reserve furnishes 14 percent of the Air Force's total force at a cost of 4 percent of their budget and participates in fire fighting, aerial spray missions, hurricane hunting, search and rescue, and special operations. There is still a strong competitive spirit between active duty and reserve force personnel, but there is also the realization that they are brothers/sisters in the greatest fighting force the world has ever known.

Over the years there have been numerous proposals to merge the National Guard into one reserve force similar to that employed by the Canadians. The Air Guard is somewhat vulnerable since it is not a part of the old militia heritage, having originated in 1947 when the US Air Force was established. (There are some who claim that the air arm of the National Guard came into being in 1910 when the New York Army

National Guard's First Signal Company purchased an aircraft with funds they raised on their own.) There are also claims that the Air Guard has no state function whatsoever. While this may be technically true, I well remember the many trips we flew during the (Los Angeles) Watts riots to bring military assistance to an overwhelmed police force. I can only imagine what would have transpired had it been necessary for the governor of California to apply to the Department of Defense for help. On the negative side is the claim that the Guard is heavily politicized and flawed with incompetence and cronyism. Based on my own experience, I felt that for the most part, we had excellent personnel (both officer and airman) at the working level, but I would agree with the criticism when applied to command and administrative functions. This was the observation that motivated me to begin developing a plan to eliminate dead wood and create a road map for officer advancement. If the Air Guard cannot overcome the management shortfall, I then concur that it should be merged into the AF Reserve structure (comprised of thirty-five wings, five groups, and seventy-three squadrons), where there are no governors to circumvent or shortcut the promotion system. In any event, both the Air Guard and the AF Reserve have become an indispensable element in the air force inventory.

REMINISCING

As I review my life, there were many forks in the road, any one of which would have resulted in a major change in my life and in my chosen career. I was never content with the status quo and was constantly alert for schools, extra training, or other opportunities to broaden my experience and background. Consequently, there were always options. I consistently chose to reach a bit beyond my current expertise to facilitate future personal development. As I moved into command positions, I looked for the same attitude in subordinates, and I would watch for opportunities to assign projects to them which would enhance their experience level.

Lt. D is an excellent example of how courage, tenacity, and refusal to quit can offset a plethora of negative factors on the rocky road to a goal. Accepting funds from his parents' savings so that he could attend dental school created an added pressure that surely haunted him daily. Fortunately, Lt. D had an extra helping of self-confidence, a keen sense of responsibility, and a reverent regard for personal accountability.

DH is another successful example. He is a third generation owner of an upscale clothing store in my hometown. The business was founded by his grandfather in 1902 and passed on to DH's father in 1928. In the early 1930s, DH started working for the store, folding cardboard packing boxes in anticipation of weekend sales. He has been there ever since. Over the years, business prospered, and when DH succeeded his father as the owner, he believed it was time to bring the store into the new millennium. He was aware that a local shoe store was using the Internet quite successfully for marketing, and he began to speculate as to how it might be applied to the clothing and dry cleaning business. He retained TF who worked for a firm that specialized in placing businesses online, and in the first month DH's website got seven thousand hits. The rest is history. He now ships clothing internationally and has added four employees to keep up with orders. On a recent visit, I found him preparing a shipment of one hundred ties to a Saudi sheik!

As I appraise my life and that of Lt. D and DH, I am impressed with the similarity of events that shaped our lives. Lt. D faced a multitude of incidents over a relatively short period of time—any one of which would have changed his life forever and posed dire financial consequences for his family. His passionate dream to succeed at dentistry and rock solid tenacity were the backbone of his achievements. However, he needed the "breaks" he got along the way and a portion of luck to round out his success.

DH's success was less tenuous. He took a well-established business, and rather than let it rest on it's laurels, visualized something better. As he moved into Internet sales, he added his own innovations (i.e., free shipping) and the business mushroomed (however, he continued to operate from the modest location established by his father and grandfather). If you call that store today, you may hear DH on the other end of the line. The inevitable conclusion is that by following his dream, DH avoided the fate of a competing store that has since gone out of business.

In my own case, I loved and respected the flying business and constantly reached for total involvement. And there is no doubt that I had a lot of help and my share of luck along the way. There are those who say that you make your own luck; however, I cannot help but recognize that a lot of my luck was well beyond my ability to engender.

I owe so much to so many people—especially the two families that were always there for me. First, of course my mother and father. Although they did not always agree with me, they were always there to lend whatever support they could. I've never forgotten that my mother worked long, hard hours in the house— cooking, cleaning, and washing, and then lending a hand in the fields or caring for the livestock—and all those times when she worked late into the evening making or patching clothing so that her children would always be neat and clean. My memories of Mother and Dad and my sense of indebtedness will always be a huge part of my life (and here I have to note that it took me twenty years before I could discuss my father's passing without tearing up). I am equally indebted to my children and their mother who spent hours waiting for me to return from lengthy absences, while many of my responsibilities around the house and yard fell into their laps. As hard as I might try, I wasn't always available to watch my son play baseball or catch the girls' dance recitals. It is easy to justify these disappointments as the consequence of "doing it for them." There probably is some truth to that, but by no stretch of the imagination would I categorize it as pure benevolence.

In the final analysis, my greatest accomplishment is the love of my family and the respect of so many remarkable people that I worked with. Among my most cherished awards are a couple of letters from members of my former command. One of them wrote, "You were one of the good guys," and another wrote, "You were tough, but you were fair." One gentleman wrote that it was easy to work for me because there was never a question about where I stood on any given matter.

What more could I ask for?

Epilogue

I firmly believe that I have lived my life in the best of times. There will be some in today's world who might feel that I was robbed of a childhood because of the responsibilities assigned to me at an early age. Nothing could be further from the truth. I loved working with the farm machinery, and while some of the tasks around the farmstead were a bit of a drudge, they were part of a package my parents and I shared. I have no doubt that the first sixteen years of my life were critical in shaping the person I became.

There was always work to be done, and I learned that procrastination stole time from other things that needed attention. I was eighteen when I developed a philosophy that has served me well. My father and I were building a fence when we ran short of supplies, and Dad had to go into town to buy the needed items. I continued to work in the July heat but was sorely tempted to seek the shade and comfort of a nearby grove of trees. Finally, reality caught up with me, and I reminded myself, "This fence has to be built. There is no one to do the job except Dad and me, and he isn't here right now, so I need to get on with it." There have been hundreds of times in my life where this maxim has prevailed. For example, when involved in office work, I made it a practice that once something was removed from my in-basket, it would rarely be returned (some of my associates nicknamed me "Mr. Now").

Most people have capabilities well beyond their operating level. If those capabilities are to be utilized, you must have a dream or goal. Then you must have confidence in yourself, courage, tenacity, and the ability to suffer reversals, hardship, and even failure. It is essential that you love your work and that you engage it to the very best of your ability. Take advantage of every opportunity to broaden and expand your expertise. Objectivity is a vital element in all events, especially as you examine your own performance. Loyalty to subordinates, peers, a boss, and the company you work for is crucial. Be a good listener and do not hesitate to render an honest opinion when one is called for. Maintain an open mind and be alert for ideas at all levels within your company, industry, and related fields, and give public attribution to those who contribute to your success. Finally, take care of your work, and it will take care of you.

Postscript

On June 12, 2005 (my eighty-second birthday), I went skydiving (a gift from my son, Greg) with my three grandsons and youngest daughter, Judy.

Work hard but take some time to play as you go.

Life is short. It is sweet. Go get it.

ADDENDUM

1. Riverside Residence
2. Hurt Farm Supply
3. Kingsley Residence
4. Grandpa Hurt's house
5. the original Multispread

1--DePauw Univ--1952

2--Circa 1977

3, 4--Korea-1952

1. DePauw University Military Staff
2. The Author
3. Active Duty: Korea

```
77 SEP 02                          INDIVIDUAL FLIGHT                        PAGE   02 OF 77 NOV 01  PLT
HUNT OSCAR A                        ASC: 7S  EFFECTIVE: 74 JAN 01 AC: 3 CMD-ASGND:   MAC  CMD-ACFT: MAC  ACFT/BAC:  C13
8-0              CURR-ARU-RT:CMD PLT   ORG-RT-DT: 6N NOV 04 PI: 6 FLY-ORGN:   0146  SQ: P  CR:   PGI/DATE:
478-26-4750      ADDN-ARU-RT:NONE      ADD-RT-DT:          ISA: Y FLT-REC-LDE: XTBT  OP-LOC:  XTBT  BASE: VAN NUYS
1 SEP 30  ASD: 49 SEP 30  SERV-CATS: NBRSBN ACFT=N  ACIP-DN-FLYING:  NOT COMPUTED - ASD IS PRIOR TO 1 JAN 1956
```

R/DAYS	TAIL	MSN	DUTY	TOTAL	DAY		NIGHT		IML	TRAIN	LANDINGS			PENT	APPR	NMBR OF	LOC
		SYM	POSN		VFR	IRST	VFR	INST	NAT	SIM	TYPE AND NMBR	S	B	P	N	SORTIES	US
C130E	839	T30	FP	.45	.2			.8			LL			1		1	000
C130E	826	T30	CP	4.0	4.0									1	1		000
C130E	826	T30	FP	4.5	4.0			.5			LL 1			1	1		000
C130E	433	T30	FP	1.0	.5			.5			LL 1 TG 2			2		1	001
C130E	433	T30	AC	1.5	1.5												001
C1305	755	T30	FP					2.4			LL 3			1	1	2	002
				14.9	12.6			1.7			7			3	3	5	

TOT-PLT	I/PLT	CG-PLT	CMD-PLT	EVAL-PLT	OTHER	TOT-PLT	STUD	CIV	OTH-US	FGN-MIL	GRND-TOT	CMBT	C
8.5		4.0			1.5	14.3					14.3		
2906.1	4317.4	1470.0	197.1		249.5	9465.1	107.0	2908.0			11701.1		

Final page –AF Flight record

The Author (Circa 1977)

Sky diving

Skydiving

The author and T-6, circa 2005

The author and AT-6

Lt D and airplane

Boeing 747

Schilling AFB

Boeing B-47

UAL Boeing 747

Lockheed C-130

C-130 Cockpit

Lockheed C-130

Cockpit Boeing C-97

Boeing C-97

March Field, circa 1940

Van Nuys airport

"The Big Easy"